CARMELITE BIBLE MEDITA...
TRULY THE SON OF ...
The Way of the Cross in the Gospel...

BY JOSEPH CHALMERS, O.CARM.

TRULY THE SON OF GOD

The Way of the Cross in the Gospel of Mark

Joseph Chalmers, O.Carm.
With a foreword by Cardinal Keith O'Brien

Saint Albert's Press & Edizioni Carmelitane
2012

© British Province of Carmelites.

All rights reserved. Except as permitted under current legislation no part of this work may be photocopied or reproduced, stored in a retrieval system, published, performed in public, adapted, broadcast, transmitted, recorded or reproduced in any form or by any means without the prior permission of the copyright owner.

The right of Joseph Chalmers to be identified as the author of this work has been asserted in accordance with sections 77 and 78 of the Copyright, Designs and Patents Act 1988.

The British Province of Carmelites does not necessarily endorse the individual views contained in its publications.

First published 2012 by Saint Albert's Press & Edizioni Carmelitane.

Saint Albert's Press
Whitefriars, 35 Tanners Street,
Faversham, Kent, ME13 7JN, United Kingdom
www.carmelite.org
ISBN-10: 0-904849-44-9
ISBN-13: 978-0-904849-44-8

Edizioni Carmelitane
Centro Internationale S. Alberto
Via Sforza Pallavicini, 10
00193 Roma, Italy
www.carmelites.info/edizioni
ISBN-13: 978-88-7288-125-5

Edited and designed by Johan Bergström-Allen, T.O.C.
Carmelite Projects & Publications Office, York.

Typeset by Jakub Kubů, Prague, Czech Republic.
Printed by ERMAT Praha s.r.o., Czech Republic.
Production coordinated by Karmelitánské nakladatelství s.r.o.,
Kostelní Vydří 58, 380 01 Dačice, Czech Republic, www.kna.cz.

Copyright notices for the various publications cited in this book are included in the footnotes. All reasonable attempts to seek copyright permissions have been made; if, inadvertently, any copyright infringements have been made, these will be corrected in future editions.

Saint Albert's Press would like to thank the Carmelite friar communities at Aylesford and Faversham, England, for permission to reproduce images. Photography is by Kevin Melody, O.Carm., and Johan Bergström-Allen, T.O.C.

CONTENTS

Foreword 7

Introduction 9

First Station: Conspiracy against Jesus (*Mark* 14:1-11) 19

Second Station: Preparations for the Last Supper (*Mark* 14:12-16) 29

Third Station: Jesus is betrayed (*Mark* 14:17-31) 37

Fourth Station: In Gethsemane (*Mark* 14:32-52) 49

Fifth Station: Before the Sanhedrin (*Mark* 14:53-65) 61

Sixth Station: Peter denies Jesus (*Mark* 14:66-72) 71

Seventh Station: Pilate condemns Jesus (*Mark* 15:1-15) 81

Eighth Station: Jesus is crowned with thorns (*Mark* 15:16-20a) 93

Ninth Station: The way of the cross (*Mark* 15:20b-21) 101

Tenth Station: The crucifixion (*Mark* 15:22-27) 109

Eleventh Station: Jesus is mocked on the cross (*Mark* 15:29-32) 119

Twelfth Station: Jesus dies on the cross (*Mark* 15:33-37) 127

Thirteenth Station: Reaction to the death of Jesus (*Mark* 15:38-41) 137

Fourteenth Station: The burial of Jesus (*Mark* 15:42-47) 149

Fifteenth Station: The empty tomb (*Mark* 16:1-8) 159

Select Bibliography 167

The Carmelite Family in Britain 170

Carmel on the Web 172

The Carmelite Institute of Britain & Ireland (CIBI) 173

Other titles available 174

Also available in the Carmelite Bible Meditations series 175

FOREWORD

Each one of us needs help in our prayer – and it is a joy to see again this help provided by Father Joseph Chalmers, the former Prior General of the Carmelite Order.

Following on his books of Biblical meditations on the prophet Elijah and Our Lady, Father Joseph has this time written a set of meditations on the Passion of Our Lord, entitled *Truly the Son of God*. We are all familiar with the 'Stations of the Cross'. This book takes St. Mark's Gospel and, inspired by the 'Stations', gives reflections on fifteen episodes of the Passion of the Lord. The reflections are based not just on Sacred Scripture but also on the Christian contemplative tradition, particularly in this book, on the teachings of St. Teresa of Avila.

Father Joseph stresses that "each Station will name the part of the story of the Passion that the text describes. Therefore, the Stations do not always follow the traditional fourteen that you may know, but they do tell the story exactly as Mark told it". I think that is one of the strengths of this book – we are brought back to the words of Sacred Scripture themselves and, quoting a book on the 'Stations of the Cross' published at Nuremberg in 1521, we are told "it is much better to make pilgrimage with one's heart than with one's feet".

The method which Father Joseph uses in this book is effectively that of *Lectio Divina*, the ancient way to immerse oneself in the Word of God. After a section in each Station called *Reading* there is a section entitled *Reflecting*, followed by *Responding*, then *Resting*. Regarding the final section of each Station, entitled *What's Next?*, Father Joseph rightly states that prayer is important, but if it is authentic it will have an effect on our daily lives!

Consequently, you will realise that these are pointed reflections on fifteen different episodes of the Passion of Our Lord. This is indeed a book not just for Lent but for any time we wish to indulge in guided prayer throughout the year.

I recommend this book to those who wish to immerse themselves in the account of the Passion of Our Lord from St. Mark's Gospel, thus strengthening their own Christian faith and their desire for Christian action.

+ Cardinal Keith Patrick O'Brien
Archbishop of St. Andrews & Edinburgh

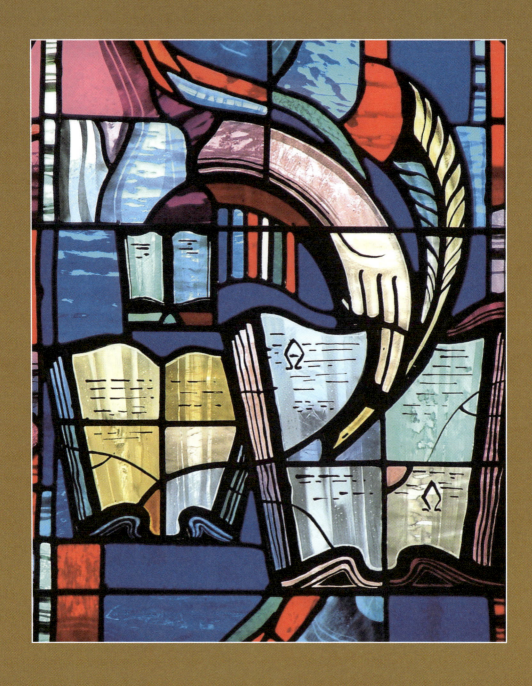

The writing of the Word of God.
Window by George Walsh in the Chapel of Avila Discalced Carmelite Friary, Dublin.

INTRODUCTION

In the heart of Jerusalem late one spring morning in a year between 30 and 33 A.D., a small group of Roman soldiers and others escorted some condemned men to their appointed place of execution, named by the Roman occupiers "Calvary". The men carried the cross beam on which they would be nailed and which would be attached to the vertical beam already in place awaiting them. It was not the first such procession and it would not be the last, but it certainly became the most famous. Jesus of Nazareth, an itinerant preacher, had become bothersome to the powers that be and had to pay the price. The Romans had found crucifixion to be a useful weapon in their subjugation of the many peoples that formed their empire. It was horrifying, principally for the one condemned to die in such a cruel way, but it was also intended to horrify the onlookers in order to dissuade them from running the risk of paying the same price.

The death of Jesus was not the end. He was buried in a tomb and the stone was rolled in place, but early on the Sunday morning some of the women who had followed him and ministered to him on his journeys experienced something that amazed and initially terrified them. The stone had been rolled away and there was no sign of the body! He had risen from the dead! Jesus was the long-awaited Messiah and had been constituted Lord of the world. The disciples went all over the world to proclaim the Good News of God's powerful intervention in human history in the resurrection of His Son.

From very early times pilgrims went to visit the land where Jesus lived and died. They sought to retrace the steps of the small group that had originally escorted the condemned man to Calvary as he stumbled to his death. There is an enduring story that Saint Helena, the mother of the Roman Emperor Constantine, found the true cross in the environs of Jerusalem around the year 326. Since then relics of the true cross have multiplied!

The 'Stations of the Cross' is a very well-known and popular devotion that is practised especially during the Lenten season. There are numerous published Stations of the Cross to help people follow Christ's passion and they range from the devotional to those that try to make the events of 2000 years ago have an immediate impact on the social issues of the day. Every Catholic church throughout the world has its own version of the Stations, some of more artistic value than others. Every Good Friday night large crowds flock to the Coliseum in Rome to follow the Way of the Cross with the Pope. The meditations are usually prepared by an eminent theologian or biblical scholar. It is interesting to note that a recently beatified Carmelite friar, Blessed Angelo Paoli, was the first to think of placing a cross in the Coliseum in Rome. Of course no pilgrimage to the Holy Land would be complete without following what is presumed to have been the path that Jesus himself took from Pilate's residence in Jerusalem to the place of execution. Usually the Via Dolorosa is a scene of utter confusion that may very well have been similar to the scene on that first Good Friday.

My intention in this book is to seek to retell the story of the Passion of Jesus, from the standpoint of Mark's Gospel, helped by the insights of some great biblical scholars of our day, and then to see how these insights might affect our relationship with God and with other people. Most scholars, although by no means all, accept the idea that Mark's Gospel was the first to be written and that the Gospels of Matthew and Luke borrow heavily from it. Three quarters of Mark's Gospel can be found in both the other two, and there is only a tiny portion of Mark's Gospel that cannot be found in either Matthew's or Luke's version of the Good News. These three Gospels are called the *Synoptics* because they see things through the same lens, as it were. John's Gospel has a different approach to the story but nevertheless has several features in common with the others.

There are differences in the various Gospel presentations of the central mystery of the Christian faith. There are, of course, all sorts of theories as to how the Gospels came to be written. If Mark's Gospel is the first, the author did not just dream up all the bits that go to make up the document; he had a number of sources on which he drew, many of these were stories that had been passed on by word of mouth or were used when the community gathered together in prayer. He also had a plan of what he wanted to say and how he wanted to say it. With all these ideas and stories and memories of Jesus, he wove a document that would bring the Good News about Jesus Christ, the Son of God, to the ends of the earth. When Matthew and Luke came to write their Gospels, it is thought that they had a written version of Mark in front of them as well as other sources. John's Gospel has some connection with the other three, but also had access to other traditions that give a different slant to the same story, and he wanted to present it in a completely fresh way.

The approach to each Station will be to focus on a particular piece of Scripture from the Gospel according to St. Mark, and to try to open its riches using the method of *Lectio Divina,* the ancient way to immerse oneself in the Word of God. The text will be taken from one of the modern translations, and I will vary these as we go through the book. It is useful to read a story with which we are very familiar but is put in an unfamiliar way. Sometimes this will jolt us into seeing it with new eyes. If you follow all the Stations of the Cross in this book, you will have read the whole of the story of the Passion of Jesus in Mark's Gospel. I have started with the scene at the supper in Bethany when Jesus is anointed and when the final decision is taken to do away with him. We will end with the scene at the empty tomb.

The method of *Lectio Divina*, or prayerful reading of the Scriptures, starts off simply by reading the text. After the text itself, there will be a section in each Station called '**Reading**'. In this part I try to clarify what the story is about, and point out some interesting elements of it. Next comes a section entitled '**Reflecting**', and here I try to apply the particular part of the story of the Passion to our lives today, but of course that is only a small start. Each one of us must continue this reflection throughout our lives and apply the Gospel in the particular situation in which we find ourselves. I have also used my own imagination to describe the scene from the perspective of a participant, who may or may not be mentioned in the particular passage of Scripture. This section is given the title of the particular person who is meant to be speaking. Another section follows which I have called '**Responding**', and here each of us is encouraged to take time to respond to God in our own way and this will usually emerge from what has preceded it. I will try to kick start a response. After all that we might need a rest, and so appropriately the next section is called '**Resting**'. Here I will talk about some of the issues we might come across, especially in prayer, when we seek to follow Jesus faithfully. I have been shaped by my own formation as a Carmelite, and much of what I say will have a Carmelite tinge. Another section is entitled '**What's next?**'; prayer is important, but if it is authentic it will have an effect on our daily lives, so I will try to give some pointers as to how we might make sure that our prayer is translated into action.

Each Station will name the part of the story of the Passion that the text describes. Therefore the Stations do not always follow the traditional fourteen that you may know but they do tell the story exactly as Mark told it. My intention is that these little scenes might open up a different way of looking at what happened to Jesus and examine our own response to him. The traditional devotion of the Stations of the Cross is an ideal way into deepening the relationship with Christ as we seek to understand what he has done for us. We also learn from this devotion what is implied in the title "follower of Christ".

INTRODUCTION

The artistic representation of the Stations come mostly from the Polish artist, Adam Kossowski, whose work embellishes the shrine of the Carmelite friars at Aylesford Priory in England. All the photographs, including those of the Stations, were kindly taken by Kevin Melody, O.Carm.

When I cite the odd verse of Scripture throughout the book, I use a variety of translations and sometimes the quote comes from memory. I check the accuracy of my memory, but sometimes I cannot quite remember which translation it comes from. I hope that does not distract you too much, but you can always try to hunt it down for yourself.

The History of the Devotion

The 'Stations of the Cross' are a pilgrimage in miniature to Jerusalem. It is only in the past forty years or so that travel to foreign parts became possible for those of modest means. For most people a pilgrimage to Jerusalem to see the places associated with Jesus was unthinkable. The devotion of the Stations of the Cross brought Jerusalem – and especially where Jesus had suffered and died – into every church and allowed every follower of Christ to meditate on the sufferings which he had undergone for the salvation of the world.[1]

The *Via Dolorosa*, the street in Jerusalem which Christians named to honour the painful journey of Jesus from Pilate's palace to Calvary, was perhaps even in the Emperor Constantine's time (the early fourth century) a place of pilgrimage for those few intrepid travellers from Europe who faced the perilous journey over land and sea. The name of the street is much later, perhaps even from as late as the fifteenth or sixteenth century. Doubt has been cast over whether this was indeed the route taken by Jesus to his death. However, certainly in the fourth century there was a significant Christian population in Jerusalem and this community apparently believed it to be important to keep a faithful record of where Jesus had lived, died and rose again. Of course from this period of history documents are distinctly lacking, and so any statement is open to criticism and correction from subsequent generations. However, our intention is not to verify the site of the holy places in Jerusalem but simply to point out that the devotion of the Stations of the Cross began as a spiritual pilgrimage to the city where Jesus died and rose again.

---

1 Much of the information for the pre-history of our modern Stations of the Cross is taken from a book dating from 1906: Herbert Thurston, *The Stations of the Cross: An Account of their History and Devotional Purpose*, (London: Burns & Oates, 1906).

There are documents which claim that Our Lady, the Blessed Virgin Mary, would go each day to the places associated with her Son's Passion, death and resurrection. The pilgrims who managed to reach the Holy Land would do the same. The immediate antecedents of the devotion of the Stations of the Cross are the constructions of pious pilgrims of the fourteenth and fifteenth centuries, when they returned home, which were intended to represent the holy places of Jerusalem. They used these to follow the Lord's path of suffering in various ways. The word 'Stations' seems to be used for the first time in relation to the places in Jerusalem which were associated with Jesus' journey of suffering in the middle of the fifteenth century by a pilgrim from Eton College in England. The earliest known Stations of the Cross are the carvings in Nuremberg. They were probably completed around 1490 and have been restored several times. They were originally seven in number. Later in the Low Countries these are expanded to fifteen or sixteen stations, published in books with woodcuts and meditations. In an early sixteenth-century book of meditations on Christ's Passion, the author states: "Every man can erect these Stations in his own house. A simple cross will serve to mark them ... It is much better to make pilgrimage with one's heart than with one's feet."[2]

In another book, published in 1563, the Carmelite author gives meditations for the whole year, and in the midst of these we can find our modern fourteen Stations of the Cross in the order well known to us.[3] The selection of the Stations owes much more to the pious ingenuity of devotional writers in Europe than to the actual practice of pilgrims to Jerusalem. The great flourishing of the devotion owes much to the dedication of the Franciscans who have had care of the holy places in Jerusalem for several hundred years. Some of the scenes we are accustomed to in the Stations of the Cross have Scriptural warrant, and others none. The scene where Veronica wipes the face of Jesus, or where Jesus meets his mother on the way to the cross, come from the imagination of spiritual writers of the sixteenth century and are not mentioned in the Gospel accounts. What is important is that we are led to prayer. As Thurston says in his history of the Stations of the Cross, "If one particular set of Stations has prevailed in preference to another, this, I conceive, is ultimately to be attributed to the fact that the one appeals more strongly to the pious imagination or to the devotional needs and feelings of the faithful at large."[4]

---

2   From a book published in 1521 at Nuremberg cited in *The Stations of the Cross, ibid.*, p. 82.
3   Jan Pascha, *La Pérégrination Spirituelle*, Louvain, ed. Peter Calentyn, 1563, cited in *The Stations of the Cross, ibid.*, pp. 82-86.
4   Thurston, *The Stations of the Cross, ibid.*, pp.136-137.

INTRODUCTION

The Story of the Passion

The Passion of Jesus from his arrest to his burial is the longest piece in each Gospel.[5] It is central to the whole Christian story. No one wrote an eye witness account of the Passion and death of Jesus. What we have are four different accounts written between thirty and seventy years after the events. They all tell the same story but from different perspectives that emerge from the way each Evangelist has decided to structure his gospel and from the sources that were available to him. There is great debate as to whether one of the main sources for the Gospel writers was a pre-existing account of the Passion of Jesus. All of the Gospel writers are profoundly affected by their faith in the resurrection, that is, they are not just telling a story of a dead hero whom they admired. They are proclaiming that Jesus is Lord and is risen from the dead. Towards the end of John's Gospel, the writer explains that he could have written much more but he chose what to write "so that you may believe that Jesus is the Christ, the Son of God, and that believing this, you may have life through his name" (*John* 20:31). The other Evangelists might well have written something similar.

I will take Mark's Gospel as my guide in what follows, but I may digress here and there where we come across something particularly interesting. The Passion account in Mark's Gospel takes up two lengthy chapters which is a very considerable proportion of the whole Gospel, but the Passion is prepared for in a much wider context. Someone has said that the Gospels are Passion stories with lengthy introductions. While that is an exaggeration, it does make the point that the Passion of Jesus is a very important part of all four Gospels. These accounts seem to have been in existence earlier than the other bits of the Gospels. There are very many Old Testament themes running through the Gospels and particularly in the story of the Passion of Jesus. The first Christians were faced with the unenviable task of proclaiming that the poor soul who was tortured and killed in the cruellest way was, in fact, the long-awaited Messiah of Israel. More than that, Jesus rose again from the dead and is now Lord of all creation. In him every human being is invited to become a member of God's People. The first Christians looked back to the Old Testament to find there prophecies and ideas that pointed towards what had happened to Jesus the Christ. Through pondering some of the prophecies and themes of the Old Testament, the early Christians were able to get over the scandal of the cross

---

[5] The most profound study so far of the passion in all four Gospels is that of Raymond E. Brown, 'The Death of the Messiah' in *The Anchor Bible Reference Library*, 2 volumes, (Geoffrey Chapman, 1994). In the preface to volume one, Brown says that he spent at least ten years on this book and he includes seventy pages of bibliography. Brown's scholarship in biblical matters is unparalleled, and so I am happy to refer anyone who is interested to his two volume masterpiece. Hereinafter this work will be referred to as *Brown* with the volume and page number given.

and understand that what had happened to Jesus was in fact according to God's will and the divine plan for the salvation for all people.

It is significant that in the story of the Passion, John is quite similar to the other three Gospels, while in the other parts he diverges considerably. Mark begins his version of the Good News by stating what the point of the Gospel is: "The beginning of the Good News of Jesus messiah, Son of God". The centre point of Mark's Gospel is Peter's profession of faith at Caesarea Philippi in chapter 8 (verses 27-30). Jesus asks the vital question, "Who do you say that I am?". Peter answered for all the disciples saying that he believed Jesus to be the Christ, that is, the anointed messiah that Israel had been awaiting for centuries. The first eight chapters have been leading up to this profession of faith because they have been a gradual unfolding of the mystery of the person of Jesus. Now we come to the point where he is recognised as the messiah by Peter. The next eight chapters are the teasing out of what it means to call Jesus the Christ or the messiah. Three times Jesus predicts his own suffering, death and resurrection (8:31; 9:31; 10:33) and the disciples either reject the idea or do not understand what he is talking about.

Immediately after the profession of faith there is a very strange sentence: "He gave them strict orders not to tell anyone about him". This is strange indeed because surely Jesus came to preach the Good News of the Kingdom of God to all peoples? This is clarified, I think, in what follows. Jesus prophesies for the first time that he will suffer and die. Peter tries to get Jesus back on the right path and he suffers a stinging rebuke for his pains. Jesus calls him a "Satan", or a serious stumbling block, "because the way you think is not God's way but man's" (8:33). Then Jesus makes abundantly clear the uncompromising condition of following him, and the scene of the Transfiguration where the Law and the Prophets represented by Moses and Elijah give backing to Jesus' own understanding of his mission. The final seal comes with the voice from the cloud, which says, "This is my Son, the Beloved. Listen to Him." (*Mark* 9:8).

So the disciples are to remain quiet for the moment about who Jesus is because they must learn what it means for Jesus to be the messiah. The lesson will be painful in the extreme. Jesus will be a suffering messiah – the suffering servant of the Lord, the Son of God who is revealed precisely at the moment of his final degradation, when he hangs dead on the cross. Anyone who wishes to follow Christ must throw in his lot with him. The follower must be prepared to suffer with Christ in order to share his glory.

INTRODUCTION

Mark's message is uncompromising and stark. He and his community of fellow Christians faced the problem of trying to find some meaning in the absurd events of the passion and perhaps in various persecutions they themselves had been through. Could the definitive revelation of God be this poor Galilean preacher who was executed as a common criminal? Mark's answer to this question is *Yes*. The key to the understanding of Mark's Gospel is the person of Jesus as Son of God. This is especially the case for the Passion. Throughout the Passion narrative we have indications here and here that what is happening is being used by God to bring about a greater purpose. Mark's message has great similarities to that of St. Paul who preached the scandal and the foolishness of the cross which showed God's eternal wisdom. The Son of God is revealed when he has plumbed the depths of human suffering. Anyone who wants to follow Christ must be prepared to do what he did.

In Mark's Gospel, Jesus fuses the glorious notion of the Son of Man from the prophet Daniel with the figure of the Suffering Servant from the Prophet Isaiah. The messiah is indeed a glorious figure but first of all it is necessary for him to suffer and die. Glory is won at great cost. Discipleship costs not less than everything. The great opposition to Jesus does not come as a shock at the end of the Gospel. We have already been told that there was an earlier plot to destroy him (*Mark* 3:20) and Jesus does nothing to lessen the opposition. He faces his passion and cross as his destiny, which will be used by God to save all the people.

When we read the Gospels we have to remember that we are faced with ancient documents. This is crucial because we must not be surprised that the writers do not have the same interests that we have, nor do they have the same questions. We might like to know exactly what were the objections to Jesus, what was the motivation of Judas and so on. However, when we read any book, we have to understand that the author might have a different mindset to ours and this is particularly the case with an ancient text. The Gospel writers presume a knowledge of what we now call the Old Testament and they often want to show that the life, and particularly the death of Jesus fulfils the biblical prophecies. Our knowledge of the Bible is often not quite so detailed and so I have tried to point out when there is a particularly important allusion to the Old Testament in one of the scenes of the Passion. The psalms, which formed the prayer book of Israel, will come up often in the account of the Passion. I have used them also to try to lead us into a deeper awareness of the presence of God in our lives as we go through the different events that make up the account of the Passion of Jesus.

The Gospels were very probably written back to front in the sense that the first story to be developed is that of the Passion, death and resurrection of Jesus. The first preaching about Jesus was to Jewish people and the preachers had to answer an obvious objection: How can this man who was executed as a blasphemer be the long awaited messiah? The followers of Jesus had to show how this was according to God's plan as displayed in the Scriptures. Other memories about what Jesus said and did were added until each Evangelist put these stories into a structure that responded to the questions and situation of his own community.

We have our own questions and situations. Let us now seek to follow Jesus on his path of suffering to see whether this story might help us see some light and live our faith more profoundly.

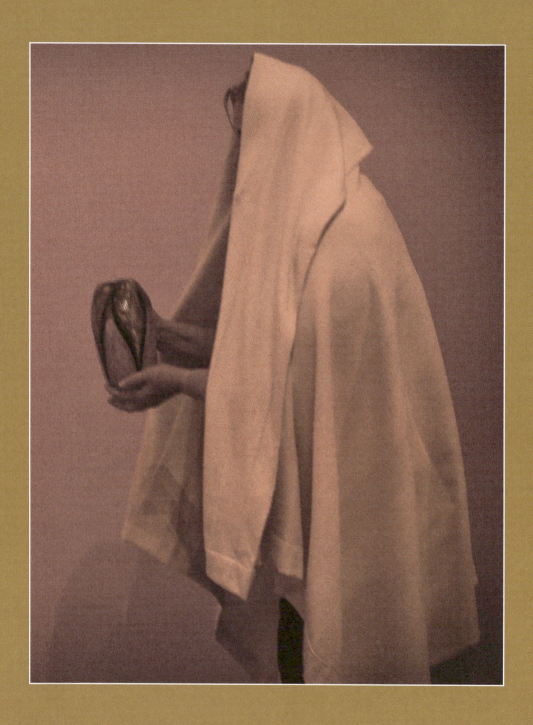

'A woman came with an alabaster jar of very costly ointment of nard,
and she broke open the jar and poured the ointment on Jesus' head.'
(Mark 14:3)

The First Station

CONSPIRACY AGAINST JESUS

Mark 14:1-11

We are going to follow Jesus through his Passion according to Mark's Gospel. Let us get in the mood with the following prayer.

Prayer

O God, help me to be faithful to Jesus your Son through all the highs and lows of life. When his words challenge me, let me not turn away. Above all, let me never betray him by foolish notions or by frittering away my life in what has no lasting value. Amen.

Text

Read attentively the following text for the first time in order to get an idea of the overall sense and to take in the details. I have used the translation from the *New Revised Standard Version* (*NRSV*).[6] This is a revision of the *Revised Standard Version* (*RSV*) which dates from 1952, and was based on the *St. James Bible*, often called *The Authorised Version*. It modernises and simplifies the language of the *RSV*, as well as making the language inclusive.

> ¹ It was two days before the Passover and the festival of Unleavened Bread. The chief priests and the scribes were looking for a way to arrest Jesus by stealth and kill him; ² for they said, "Not during the festival, or there may be a riot among the people." ³ While he was at Bethany in the house of Simon the leper, as he sat at the table, a woman came with an alabaster jar of very costly ointment of nard, and she broke open the jar and poured the ointment on his head. ⁴ But some were there who said to one another in anger, "Why was the ointment wasted in this way? ⁵ For this ointment could have been sold for more than three hundred denarii, and the money given to the poor." And they scolded her. ⁶ But Jesus said,

---

[6] *The New Revised Standard Version of the Bible*, edited by Bruce M. Metzger, (New York: Oxford University Press, 1990). New Revised Standard Version Bible, copyright 1989, Division of Christian Education of the National Council of the Churches of Christ in the United States of America. Used by permission. All rights reserved.

"Let her alone; why do you trouble her? She has performed a good service for me.

⁷ For you always have the poor with you, and you can show kindness to them whenever you wish; but you will not always have me. ⁸ She has done what she could; she has anointed my body beforehand for its burial. ⁹ Truly I tell you, wherever the good news is proclaimed in the whole world, what she has done will be told in remembrance of her." ¹⁰ Then Judas Iscariot, who was one of the twelve, went to the chief priests in order to betray him to them. ¹¹ When they heard it, they were greatly pleased, and promised to give him money. So he began to look for an opportunity to betray him.

Reading

Chapter thirteen of Mark's Gospel ends with a warning by Jesus that we must all "stay awake" and immediately following we have the reason. The crisis is upon us. The passion narrative proper starts at the beginning of chapter fourteen of Mark's Gospel with the conspiracy against Jesus by the chief priests and the scribes who were looking for some way to arrest Jesus by some trick and have him put to death. Obviously he was proving very troublesome to them. Mark is at pains to point out throughout his Gospel that the death of Jesus did not simply come about through a series of errors and human sins. Jesus freely accepted his destiny as he saw it. God has become one with us and the Son of God threw in his lot with the human race. Though he was without sin, he underwent baptism at the hands of John. This was a baptism of repentance and Jesus wanted to be baptised to show his solidarity with sinful humanity. He followed this path to its logical conclusion and so he suffered the indignity of death, the humiliation of death on a cross.

We are told that the events in this scene happened two days before the feast of the Passover, which was the major event in the Jewish religious calendar. The Passover could only be properly celebrated in Jerusalem and as many as possible made a pilgrimage to the holy city for the festival. The Jewish people took over a pagan festival and gave it a new meaning associating it with the escape of the Chosen People from the slavery of Egypt. A lamb was sacrificed and eaten in memory of the night the people passed from death to life, when the Lord passed through Egypt to strike down the first born of the Egyptians and passed over the houses of the Israelites (*Exodus* 12:1-28). Unleavened bread was used for the following seven days to remind the people of their ancestors who were in a great hurry to escape from Egypt (cf. *Exodus* 12:15-20). Sometimes the whole eight days was called Passover and sometimes the feast of Unleavened Bread. This was the greatest feast of the year and looked forward to the liberation to come, which would be brought by the messiah.

The real opponents of Jesus are the leaders: the chief priests and the scribes. The Jewish priesthood was hereditary and so there were a large number of priests of different grades. At the top of the pile sat Caiaphas who was high priest from 18-36/37 A.D. The high priest was considered to be the most important political as well as religious figure in the Jewish world at the time of Jesus. He was responsible for making sure things were peaceable, otherwise the Roman authorities would step in, and that could be most unpleasant. The group that is called "the high priests" was probably a collection of aristocrats centred on Jerusalem who had positions of power in the Temple. Former high priests still retained a lot of influence. The scribes were the experts in the Jewish Law, which was believed to be God's Law. These two groups act as one and they are determined to bring down Jesus. They are not at all particular about the methods they use. They want to do it in a hurry and away from the crowds who, in general, are in favour of Jesus. Jerusalem was packed for the Passover and riots were greatly feared by the aristocracy as the Romans would react ferociously and the ruling class might lose their privileged position. Although they want to do away with Jesus quietly, Mark makes the point that they are not in charge, God is. Jesus will die at the Passover, the feast of liberation.

Jesus is in Bethany, about two miles from Jerusalem, having a meal. We have not heard of Simon the leper previously but presumably he was a friend or an admirer. Also we can safely presume that the leprosy was in the past or perhaps it was an obvious but not contagious disfigurement of the skin. Whatever the cause, Simon bore the name of leper and he may have been considered to be ritually impure, but such a detail never seemed to bother Jesus.

We are told that Jesus and the others "sat at table", however in actual fact it probably should be "reclined". It was very common at meals to stretch out on couches around a table. An unnamed woman pours precious and very expensive perfumed oil on the head of Jesus but this causes some indignation and criticism from unnamed onlookers. The other Gospels have a similar scene of anointing, although they use it for different purposes (*Matthew* 26:6-13; *Luke* 7:36-50; *John* 12:1-8). The woman breaks the alabaster jar which held the perfumed oil. The breaking of the jar might signify the total gift that the woman makes. She does not dole out the oil drop-by-drop but pours it all out. It seems that Mark wants to extract a symbolic meaning from this story. A king's head was anointed with oil. The title "Christ", which is the Greek translation of the Jewish "messiah" means "the anointed one". Therefore Jesus is recognised as the anointed one not in the Temple by the High Priest but by this unnamed woman in the course of a meal. Jesus understands it as a preparation for his burial since the actual burial was done in haste with no time for the appropriate niceties.

We do not know who protests about this gesture, however some people at table with Jesus do. Their protests centre around the fact that this was a complete waste of a very large sum of money, which could have been put to much better use by being given to the poor. Jesus, referring to a well-known saying in the book of *Deuteronomy* (15:11), points out that they can always assist the poor, perhaps with the implication that he knows that concern for the poor is not the real reason for the criticism. He also reveals that he is not going to be around much longer but that this gesture by the unnamed woman will become famous all over the world. One of the good works in Jewish piety was to assist the poor and another was to bury the dead. It is precisely in relation to the Passion of Jesus that this little scene takes on its importance. By showing such esteem for Jesus, the woman was preparing his body for death. The expansiveness of the woman's gesture is compared to the cheap way that the enemies of Jesus, and even his friends, treat his life.

The scene in Bethany is sandwiched between two momentous decisions. The chief priests and scribes decide to silence Jesus at all costs and Judas Iscariot decides to hand him over to them. It is pointed out that Judas was one of the Twelve specially-chosen disciples who had accompanied Jesus everywhere, who had witnessed his miracles and listened to his teaching. It is impossible to tell from the story what motivated Judas. It is unlikely that the early Christians would have had any direct evidence about the plot, but it seems that they put two and two together. The way Mark tells the story invites the readers and listeners to compare the woman and Judas. Later traditions intensified the bad character of Judas.

Reflecting

Read the passage from Mark's Gospel again. What are the main points? There is the decision to stop Jesus "by stealth"; the chief priests and scribes are willing to stoop to treachery. Then we have the scene in Bethany where the woman anoints Jesus and there is an angry outburst from some others. Finally we have the sad notice that Judas makes the decision to hand Jesus over. The Gospels can be most annoying at times. We would often like to know a bit more. Who was the woman? Who were the ones who criticised her gesture? What were the motives of Judas? There are no answers to these questions. Scripture gives us what we need to know for our salvation. It is not just a story told for our entertainment.

Mark gives us some hints about the whole story of the Passion in this opening gambit. It is a mixture of evil and good motives. Jesus will be killed and will be buried without due honours, but he has already been prepared by the woman's great generosity.

Mark seems to intend that his readers and listeners ask themselves some questions about their own response to Jesus, having seen the response of the chief priests, some table companions, the woman and Judas. I am going to suggest some questions that you might think about. This is a way of reflecting more deeply on what God is saying to you through the words of the Gospel. You might like to read the same passage in your own Bible if it is different from the one I have used. Do you notice any differences that strike you? Different words are used to tell the same story but sometimes these small differences can help us understand in a new way what the original writer intended to say.

1. How do you show honour to Jesus? Do you think that is the sort of honour Jesus wants?
2. What would you want to say to Jesus if he came to eat at your house?
3. Why do you think some people were so opposed to Jesus?

Simon the leper's story

The following is how one of the characters in the scene we have just read might have been thinking. Perhaps you have other ideas.

> *Simon: Why did I invite him? Well, I knew his friends Martha, Mary and Lazarus and they obviously loved him. He used to go to their house often and just rest. I didn't see much of him when he was there. I was interested in him and in what he had to say. I held a dinner for him and I was honoured when he accepted. He came along with those disciples of his so I expected quite an evening but it was all a bit sombre. There are one or two shifty characters among them.*

> *The woman came in with the perfume and that caused a stir in itself; women don't mix with the men at table but that sort of thing*

CONSPIRACY AGAINST JESUS

did not seem to bother Jesus. It must have cost a fortune but she was very wealthy. Anyway, she broke the vase and poured the whole lot over his head! Well, that caused a bit of a commotion! Some people began to berate the woman but Jesus was enjoying it, then he said something very strange. I didn't think much about it until a few days later when his prophecy came true. He said that she had anointed him for his burial. I didn't know what to think of it all then and I am not too sure what to think of it now.

Jesus said that the woman would be famous because what she had done would be spoken about everywhere. That was certainly true. Everybody was talking about it and even more so now.

Responding

Have another read of the text from Mark's Gospel we have been considering. We have tried to understand it and we have tried to reflect on it. Now perhaps we can let go of our own thoughts and ideas, and simply speak to God from the heart. This might take any form. What do you want to say to God after having considered the Gospel story?

Perhaps the following psalm (*Psalm* 40), also from the *New Revised Standard Version* (*NRSV*) can give you a kick start. Say it slowly and then put the book down. Let your heart speak to the heart of God.

> [1] I waited patiently for the LORD; he inclined to me and heard my cry.
>
> [2] He drew me up from the desolate pit, out of the miry bog, and set my feet upon a rock, making my steps secure.
>
> [3] He put a new song in my mouth, a song of praise to our God. Many will see and fear, and put their trust in the LORD.
>
> [4] Happy are those who make the LORD their trust, who do not turn to the proud, to those who go astray after false gods.
>
> [5] You have multiplied, O LORD my God, your wondrous deeds and your thoughts toward us; none can compare with you. Were I to proclaim and tell of them, they would be more than can be counted.
>
> [6] Sacrifice and offering you do not desire, but you have given me an open ear. Burnt offering and sin offering you have not required.

> ⁷ Then I said, "Here I am; in the scroll of the book it is written of me.
>
> ⁸ I delight to do your will, O my God; your law is within my heart."
>
> ⁹ I have told the glad news of deliverance in the great congregation; see, I have not restrained my lips, as you know, O LORD.
>
> ¹⁰ I have not hidden your saving help within my heart, I have spoken of your faithfulness and your salvation; I have not concealed your steadfast love and your faithfulness from the great congregation.
>
> ¹¹ Do not, O LORD, withhold your mercy from me; let your steadfast love and your faithfulness keep me safe forever.

Resting

The next part of this movement of prayer is to rest in the Word of God. We have read the Word, reflected on it, tried to respond to it, and now is the time to rest. This is not day-dreaming but is a profound listening to what God wants to say to us in the silence of our hearts.

Silence does not come very easily to people. IPods or the next "must-have" are used, along with radio, television and general chatter, to fill our life with noise. Of course, social interaction, keeping-up with the news, and simple entertainment have their place in human life, but we do tend to exaggerate these elements so much that we never find time for silence. The Carmelite St. John of the Cross understood that some silence is essential for the relationship with God to grow. He said that God speaks always in eternal silence.[7] In order to hear God, we need some silence.

What happens when we do find some silence? Well, up come all sorts of thoughts and feelings and they swirl around our heads like pesky flies. We can learn gradually to let go of these thoughts, whatever form they take, and simply be with God with no expectations of how we should feel.

The various characters in the story we read allowed themselves to be influenced by all sorts of thoughts and feelings. We do not know why Simon the leper invited Jesus to his house. From the beginning of the Gospel of Mark we have seen that the religious authorities have been plotting against Jesus. Obviously they cannot take any more and they are determined "to arrest Jesus by stealth

---

[7] *Sayings* 100, in K. Kavanaugh and O. Rodriguez, *The Collected Works of St. John of the Cross*, (Washington D.C.: ICS Publications, 1991). There is another older translation of the complete works: E.A. Peers, *The Complete Works of St. John of the Cross*, (London: Burns & Oates, 1954, reprinted Wheatampstead: Anthony Clarke, 1974). In the older translation, this is quoted as *Points of Love*, p. 228.

and kill him" (*Mark* 14:1). Were they motivated by jealousy, fear, anger or some other afflictive emotion? What motivated the woman with the precious oil or those who complained at how she used it? What motivated Judas? In a profound silence, we give God the space to gently point out to us what moves us to do what we do and what is the source of these feelings. Once we know, we can do something about them.

What's Next?

There is something wrong if prayer remains inside us. To be authentic, it has to have some effect on our lives. What can you carry with you from your reflection on the story of the woman's gesture of anointing Jesus on the head and the reactions of various people to him? In the silence have you become aware of something about yourself that you would like to keep an eye on in your own relationships with others?

As you return to your normal round of activities, ask God to help you to be aware of your reactions to people that perhaps are unhelpful in your relationships with them.

'And Jesus sent out two of his disciples and said to them,
"Go into the city, and a man will meet you carrying a ceramic water jar."'
(Mark 14:13)

The Second Station

PREPARATIONS FOR THE LAST SUPPER

Mark 14:12-16

To help you get into the mood to listen to God's Word, address yourself to God with the following prayer or perhaps you may want to make up your own prayer asking that you may really be able to hear what is necessary for you in the little story you are going to reflect on.

Prayer

Gracious and loving God, help me to respond generously to whatever Jesus asks of me even if I do not fully understand the reason. Help me to appreciate the many people who build the Kingdom with their humble service of others.

Text

This is a translation specifically done for a modern commentary on Mark's Gospel.[8] It took sixteen years to finish part two of the study where our passage is treated. Read the text slowly and carefully to make sure you know what is happening in the story.

> [12] And on the first day of the Feast of Unleavened Bread, when they sacrificed the Passover, his disciples said to him, "Where do you want us to go out and prepare, so that you may eat the Passover?" [13] And he sent out two of his disciples and said to them, "Go into the city, and a man will meet you carrying a ceramic water jar. Follow him, [14] and wherever he goes in, say to the master of the house, 'The teacher says, "Where is my lodging, where I may eat the Passover with my disciples?"' [15] "And he will show you a large upper room furnished *and prepared*; and there prepare for us." [16] And the disciples went out and went into the city, and found *it* just as he had told them; and they prepared the Passover.

---

[8] Joel Marcus, *Mark 8-16: A New Translation with Introduction and Commentary*, Volume 27A of *The Anchor Yale Bible* series, (ed.) John J. Collins, (New Haven & London: Yale University Press, 2009).

PREPARATIONS FOR THE LAST SUPPER

Reading

The scene is situated on the first day of the feast of Unleavened Bread, the day following the previous scene. All leaven or yeast was removed from the houses of the people on this day. We are told that this is also the day when the Passover lamb was sacrificed. This is an important reference, given what is to come, because the significance of this feast is about to be changed forever. Jesus will become the Lamb of God, sacrificed in order that all of us might pass from death to life.

The lambs were sacrificed in the outer court of the Temple and the people would eat them in their own homes. The Passover meal, strictly speaking, could only be eaten within the boundary limits of Jerusalem, although it is not all that clear whether everyone followed this exactly. Jesus sends out two of his disciples into the city to prepare everything. He is shown to be very aware of what he is doing and what is happening all around him. He is not simply the victim of forces beyond his powers but is aware that he has a destiny to fulfil. John's Gospel presents this aspect of Jesus very strongly and Mark has it to a lesser extent. The directions to the disciples were quite precise; they were to meet a man carrying a pitcher of water. The disciples found the man, went to the room, and it is just as Jesus had told them. This underlines that Jesus is in control. Presumably the owner of the house was an acquaintance of Jesus. This little scene has a great resemblance to the preparations for the triumphal entry of Jesus into Jerusalem riding on a donkey (11:1-6). Both emphasise the sovereignty of Jesus. He is in charge despite how it may appear. This may have been written to encourage Mark's own community who were suffering great persecution at the time the Gospel was written.

This was a special meal for two reasons. Firstly, it is the Passover meal which Jewish people to this day celebrate as a reminder of the time that God brought their ancestors out of the slavery of Egypt through the desert to the Promised Land. The second reason for the special nature of the meal was that it was to be the last that Jesus would celebrate with his specially-chosen disciples, the Twelve. They are the ones to whom he has entrusted his message, to whom he has taught the mysteries of the Kingdom of God. Therefore the preparations were important. Jesus is preparing to change the meaning of the Passover for those who follow him in the future by giving his body and blood to be their food and drink which would lead them to eternal life.

There is some confusion about the timing of the Passion in the Gospels. Matthew and Luke seem to follow Mark while John takes a different approach.

John wants the death of Jesus to coincide with the ritual sacrifice of the lambs. According to John, the Passover supper was held in the evening after Jesus had died, that is, the day after Mark's account. There have been all sorts of theories trying to explain this discrepancy. It is possible that Mark has interpreted the Last Supper of Jesus with his disciples as a Passover meal because of what happened later. Jesus gave himself to his disciples as their food and drink and then by his death the following day, he opened the way for them and everyone else who came after them to pass from death to life. This might be an example that ancient writers were not as concerned as we would be with exact timing, and so it is possible that John changes the timing of the Passion in order to make an important point about who Jesus is and what his mission accomplished. Another possibility is that John got it right and the other Gospels got confused with their dates since Jewish people counted the beginning of their day from sundown while the Romans counted it from midnight or even sunrise.

Reflecting

Read the Gospel passage again slowly and now we are going to try to reflect a little more deeply on it. I think that the focus of this passage is that Jesus is in control of his own destiny despite the various people who are out to bring him down. We do not know who the man carrying the water was, or the owner of the house either. The Evangelists probably knew a basic story of the Passion of Jesus and retold it in their own way but they all remained faithful to what they had received. Therefore this story about the preparations for the Last Supper seems quite banal and would probably lie on the cutting room floor of a modern film. However, Mark uses the story to emphasise that Jesus is in control. The passion and death of Jesus did not just happen. Jesus was not the helpless victim of evil as are so many people throughout the world. He was in control, and he was going to face his destiny with great courage, but before he died he wanted to share a meal with his faithful friends one last time. We know already, and we will discover later, that Jesus knew that not all were faithful. Nevertheless, he still wants to include Judas in that most significant meal.

Jesus refers to himself as "the teacher", or in some other translations as "the master", and even though there is great opposition to him there is also great devotion. In our own day many people reject religion whether out of conviction or out of apathy. Where do you stand? Presumably because you are reading this book you count yourself as a disciple of Christ. Are you willing to follow him wherever he may lead you, or do you set limits on where you will go?

PREPARATIONS FOR THE LAST SUPPER

Perhaps some of these questions might help you look a bit more deeply into the application of this text to your own life.

1. Does life just happen to you or do you think that God is at work in your life? If so, how?
2. Do you seek for what God is asking of you? If so, how?
3. Do you carry out God's will? How do you do that?

The story of the man with the pitcher

My name is Thomas. I am the house servant of a good family in Jerusalem. I went to collect water one day from the well. Usually that is Miriam's work but she had injured her hand so I went out. When I was walking home with the water jar on my shoulder I was stopped by two men. I had never seen them before. They asked me to show them the room where the teacher could eat the Passover with his disciples. I knew immediately they were talking of Jesus.

My master has a large upper room and I thought Jesus had arranged this with him so I led them to the house. It turns out that he knew nothing about it but he was very glad to welcome Jesus and his friends as he had heard him teach in the Temple and liked what he heard.

I helped set everything up but there was a sad atmosphere. When Jesus came, he thanked me. I am not used to being thanked. I just do my job. He looked at me. I will never forget that look. He looked right into my soul and he knew me. That's why I will always follow him.

Responding

Read the story in Mark's Gospel for a third time. You might like to read it in your own Bible for a change. Sometimes it is good to read the Bible in a translation that we are not used to because in this way we can be struck by unfamiliar bits of a familiar story. It is one thing to reflect on a piece of Scripture, but what might this little story say to your heart and how can you respond to God? I suggest that we try to move from head to heart now.

If you have a moment, let your heart speak to the heart of God. Do you ever ask the Lord what He wants you to do? If not, maybe you could try it now. To get you going, perhaps the following prayer of Blessed John Henry Newman might help. Say it slowly, then put the book down and spend time in the presence of God. Cardinal Newman's motto was: "Cor ad cor loquitur" – "Heart speaks to heart". Let your heart speak to the heart of God.

> *God has created me to do him*
> *Some definite service;*
> *He has committed some work to me*
> *Which he has committed no other.*
> *I have my mission ...*
> *I am a link in a chain,*
> *A bond of connection between persons.*
> *He has not created me for naught.*

Resting

When you are ready, move into silence. The point of prayer is not to tell God what He knows already or to make a list of demands. Prayer is the way we relate to God. There is a time for talking, a time for conversation, and a time for silence. We know the value of all three in any human relationships. Someone who keeps up a constant flow of chatter can become very tiresome. God, of course, is very patient, but God does desire to lead us towards a deeper level beyond the noise of words. In order to be comfortable with silence when we pray, it is a good practice to cultivate an inner silence during our normal daily life. How about turning off the mobile phone before you go into church? Do you really have to be contacted twenty-four hours a day? When you are travelling is it strictly necessary that you inform everyone around you that you are on the train? Perhaps "Mum" or whoever you are bellowing at down the phone does not possess this vital piece of information but everyone else does!

If you cannot live with silence externally, then when you come to prayer, you will not have the capacity to listen to God in the depths of your heart. Elijah, the Old Testament Prophet, experienced the presence of God in the sound of a gentle breeze or in the sound of sheer silence.[9] If you want to experience this resting in God, find little periods of silence on a regular basis. You do not have to go to extremes. Just a little bit of silence each day with no external distractions begins to prepare you to have a silent heart. This does not happen by magic or automatically; it has to be worked at. The Olympic athletes have to practice a lot before they become so good at their chosen sport. That sort

---

9 For a reflection on the stories about Elijah, see my book *The Sound of Silence: Listening to the Word of God with Elijah the Prophet*, (Faversham & Rome: Saint Albert's Press & Edizioni Carmelitane, 2007).

of level of practice is not required for prayer, but it does give us an idea that nothing comes easily. It is true, as the psalm says, that "The Lord pours his gifts on his beloved while they slumber" (*Psalm* 127:2), but in order to reach that level of rest we must learn to put a brake on some of our frenetic activity and have some external silence.

We have pondered the text in Mark's Gospel where the preparations are made for the Last Supper. Spend a moment now in silence; prepare yourself for the Lord's presence.

What's Next?

If prayer is authentic it will have some effect on our daily life. Are you prepared to meet the Lord? Christ said that whatever we did to the least, we did to him (*Matthew* 25:31-46). Perhaps today you could seek to do something for someone else without seeking any reward for yourself.

'Then Jesus took a cup, and after he had given thanks,
he passed it to them and they all drank from it. And he said,
"This is my blood of the Covenant, poured out for many".'
(Mark 14:23-24)

The Third Station

JESUS IS BETRAYED

Mark 14:17-31

Look again at the picture opposite and see all the different elements. Let us prepare to ponder the betrayal of Jesus in the context of the Last Supper in which he gave himself to his friends as their (and our) food and drink. Let us prepare to be with Jesus in this intimate moment of sharing with his friends. At this time he was betrayed.

Prayer

Dear Jesus, I thank you for the gift of yourself in the Eucharist. By receiving your body and blood I become a sharer in your divine life which will come to full flower in the eternal life in the Kingdom of your Father. Let me never forget the possibilities that exist within me of betrayal so that I may not depend on myself but on your strength. Amen.

Text

This translation is from the *Christian Community Bible*.[10] It was made specifically for the Christian communities in the Philippines but it has a much greater outreach now. It uses accessible language and has a very good introduction about the Bible, how it came to be in its present form, and how to use it. Sometimes the notes are a little questionable as they tend to interpret, rather than explain.

Read the text slowly and carefully, taking in all the different elements that go to make up this powerful story.

> [17] When it was evening, Jesus arrived with the Twelve. [18] While they were at table eating, Jesus said, "Truly, I tell you, one of you will betray me, one who shares my meal." [19] They were deeply distressed at hearing this and asked him, one after the other, "You don't mean me, do you?" [20] And Jesus answered, "It is one of you

---

[10] *Christian Community Bible: Catholic Pastoral Edition*, 48th edition, © Pastoral Bible Foundation, (Bangalore: Claretian Publications, 2010).

JESUS IS BETRAYED

Twelve, one who dips his bread in the dish with me. ²¹ The Son of Man is going, as the Scriptures say he will. But alas for that man by whom the Son of Man is betrayed; better for him if he had never been born." ²² While they were eating, Jesus took bread, blessed it and broke it, and gave it to them. And he said, "Take this; it is my body." ²³ Then he took a cup, and after he had given thanks, he passed it to them and they all drank from it. ²⁴ And he said, "This is my blood of the Covenant, poured out for many. ²⁵ Truly, I say to you, I will not taste the fruit of the vine again, until that day when I drink the new wine in the Kingdom of God." ²⁶ After singing psalms of praise, they went out to the Mount of Olives. ²⁷ And Jesus said to them, "All of you will be dismayed and fall away; for the Scripture says: 'I will strike the shepherd, and the sheep will be scattered.' ²⁸ But after I am raised up, I will go to Galilee ahead of you." ²⁹ Then Peter said to him, "Even though all the others fall away, I will not." ³⁰ And Jesus replied, "Truly, I say to you, today, this very night before the cock crows twice, you will deny me three times." ³¹ But Peter insisted, "Though I have to die with you, I will never deny you." And all of them said the same.

Reading

This supper that Jesus has with his disciples takes place in an atmosphere of tension. Judas has already taken the decision to betray the Lord and soon others will run away. Jesus announces that he will be betrayed by one of his friends and this carries an echo of *Psalm* 41:9 – "Even my closest and most trusted friend, who shared my table, rebels against me".[11] Jesus does not identify Judas here but it is clear that the act of betraying Jesus has enormous significance, especially because it is done by one of his closest companions. The psalm helped the first Christians make sense of the betrayal.

Several times Mark makes clear that the Passion is not just a dreadful event caused by the evil that people have always done to each other. It is a sign of the faithfulness of Jesus to the plan of God, which can be traced in the Scriptures. The text as we have it in verse 21 refers to Judas as the "man by whom the Son of Man is betrayed". A more exact translation is "through whom" and this

---

11 It may be interesting to note that the original says, "Even the man of my peace, the one in whom I had hoped, the one who had eaten my bread, raised up the heel against me". Most people understand the reference as being to a close and intimate friend. Nicholas King gives a powerful translation to the last part of the quote: "stabbed me in the back". See Nicholas King, *The Old Testament: A Translation of the Septuagint*, Volume 3 The Wisdom Literature, (Stowmarket, Suffolk: Kevin Mayhew Ltd., 2008), p. 90.

emphasises that Jesus is handed over to the authorities through the treachery of Judas, but God is ultimately responsible. God is in charge. Despite knowing what was ahead of him, Jesus remained faithful and went towards his destiny as a completely free man. The words of Jesus regarding the betrayer tell us nothing about the eternal fate of Judas. Jesus is condemning Judas' action. It was a typical way of underlining the gravity of what he is doing.

Then we come to the actual words of institution of the Eucharist. This section is framed by the failure of the disciples. In the New Testament we have four stories about this event: here in Mark's Gospel, then in *Matthew* 26:26-29, *Luke* 22:18-20, and *1 Corinthians* 11:23-26. Matthew and Mark are clearly following the same tradition while Luke and Paul have received and are passing on a slightly different tradition. It seems that the words and actions of Jesus were actually part of the prayer of different Christian communities from the very earliest times and they were put in as they already existed to the account of the Passion. The Gospel writers did not have complete liberty to tell the stories as they might have wanted; they received certain traditions that were venerable even in the very early days when they were composing their particular versions of the Good News about Jesus the Christ. Saint Paul makes it very clear that he is simply passing on what he himself received when he writes of the Eucharist to his Corinthian converts about the year 53 A.D. He is also not passing on a merely human tradition but he received this "from the Lord" (*1 Corinthians* 11:23). Saint John's Gospel speaks of Christ as the bread of life in chapter 6, while he replaces the words of institution at the Last Supper with the washing of the feet (*John* 13:2-15). Jesus has come to serve humanity and surely whoever receives Christ in the Eucharist must have the same sentiments.

The key words in the story of the institution of the Eucharist are the same as in two previous stories where Jesus blesses, breaks and distributes bread (*Mark* 6:30-44; 8:1-10), only this time he is giving his own life as the food of the disciples. In the traditional Passover meal the head of the family pronounced the blessing over the bread and distributed it to everyone sitting round the table. At this point Jesus changed the rite. Instead of ordinary bread, he gave to his friends his very self that he was offering for them. At the Passover the family would eat the lamb after sharing the bread. At the end of the meal they would share a traditional cup of wine. Luke and Paul tell us that Jesus took the cup after supper while Mark and Matthew omit this detail and unite the two actions. Jesus gave thanks to God and it is from this word in the original Greek that we get the term "Eucharist".

Jesus tells his disciples, who must have been a bit startled, that he was giving them his own life to be their food; he was sharing his life with them so they could come into the closest communion with him. The body and blood did not refer to a part of himself but his whole self. Jesus speaks of "my blood of the Covenant", referring to *Exodus* 24:8, where Moses ratifies the bond of love between God and the Chosen People at Sinai by sprinkling the blood of a sacrifice. This example is used in relation to the death of Jesus in the *Letter to the Hebrews* (9:19-21). The idea of covenant is crucial for understanding the whole Bible because it is the way that God expressed the divine commitment to His people. The prophets had spoken of God's constant love for the people: "I have loved you with an everlasting love" (*Jeremiah* 31:3) despite the fact that the Chosen People broke the covenant that God had made with them. The Prophet Jeremiah looked forward to a time when God would make a new covenant with the people (*Jeremiah* 31:31). The Prophet Ezekiel expresses this even more clearly when he says that the Lord will give the people a new heart in which God will place His Spirit (*Ezekiel* 36:26-28).

The covenant between God and the people was always sealed by the blood of a sacrificed animal because blood represented life. Finally Christ seals an unbreakable bond of love by the shedding of his own blood. This is why he is called the Lamb of God because he took the place of the animal that was ritually killed on the feast of Passover. The blood of the lamb was sprinkled on the doors of the Hebrew slaves in Egypt so that the angel of death would pass over them without causing harm. The death of all the firstborn in Egypt, with the exception of the Hebrew slaves, finally convinced Pharaoh to let them go (*Exodus* 12:21-34).

According to Mark, Jesus says that his blood is offered "for many". As you can imagine, there has been a lot of discussion about exactly what this means, since in English it would tend to suggest that some people might be excluded. Did Jesus only come for some people but not for others? The real experts in Scripture have studied this in detail and the best understanding of the term is that it is a Semitic expression referring to an innumerable number of individuals with no limit. Mark understands that the sacrifice of Jesus will initiate a new community that will in turn benefit every human being. There is an allusion to the mysterious figure of the Suffering Servant described in the Prophet Isaiah: "His soul's anguish over he shall see the light and be content. By his sufferings shall my servant justify many, taking their faults on himself." (*Isaiah* 53:11-12). It seems that Jesus himself interpreted his coming suffering and understood his mission to be the fulfilment of the prophecy of the Suffering Servant. Jesus has previously fed many people in the territory of Israel (*Mark* 6:34-44) and in Gentile territory (8:1-10) and now he is offering himself "for many", that is for everyone, Jew and Gentile alike. The meaning of his whole life is brought together at the Last Supper in the gift of his life.

Jesus then announces that he will not drink wine again until he drinks the new wine in the Kingdom of God. In effect this is another prophecy of his death. The first Christians celebrated the Eucharist with joyful hope of the return of Christ who would establish definitively the Kingdom of the Father. In this Kingdom, God would establish justice and harmony forever. This was often visualised in terms of a banquet. Jesus' sacrificial death is part of the divine plan that brings the Kingdom into the world.

There is a debate among Scripture scholars about whether the Last Supper was a celebration of the Passover or whether it was in fact celebrated on the night before the actual feast. However, it was certainly connected to the ritual of the Passover. There is a disagreement between John's Gospel on the one hand and the Synoptic Gospels on the other. Mark, followed by Matthew and Luke, has the crucifixion taking place on the actual feast of Passover, while John places it on the same day (Friday) but counts it as the day before the Passover. This affects the nature of the Last Supper. The Passover meal was traditionally eaten after sundown, which marked the beginning of a new day and so the beginning of the feast. The disagreement is therefore on which day did the Passover fall – on the Thursday night to Friday night (Synoptic Gospels) or the Friday night to Saturday night (John's Gospel)? According to Pope Benedict, John's timeline is safer.[12]

According to later Jewish tradition, in the rite of the Passover meal, the people normally sang Psalms 113 & 114, in which is celebrated the Passover from Egypt, that is, the escape of the Hebrew slaves from slavery. After the last cup of wine, they sang the second part (Psalms 115-118). In the Christian liturgy Psalm 118 is the Easter psalm - "this is the day that the Lord has made." The psalms that are sung at the Passover celebration are a joyful recognition of all that God has done in leading the people out of slavery. The suggestion that Pope Benedict makes is that the Last Supper was not strictly speaking a Passover meal but was a farewell meal of Jesus to his disciples. It did not necessarily follow strictly the Passover rituals but Jesus used some of these rituals to explain symbolically

---

12 Pope Benedict XVI, *Jesus of Nazareth – Part Two, Holy Week: From The Entrance Into Jerusalem To The Resurrection*, (London & San Francisco: Catholic Truth Society & Ignatius Press, 2011), pp. 106-109. Hereinafter referred to as Pope Benedict XVI, *Jesus of Nazareth*, followed by the appropriate page number.

the meaning of his life and approaching death. This was the Passover of Jesus where he took up the old rituals and brought out their full meaning.[13]

According to the Gospel story, they all sing a hymn, and then move off to the Mount of Olives where Jesus quotes the prophet Zechariah (*Zechariah* 13:7), although Mark changes the wording of the original Old Testament text, and the Lord warns the disciples that their faith will be shaken. He gives a hint of the resurrection in verse 28, but the disciples are too shaken to take that in. Peter puts on a show of bravado, denying that his faith will be shaken, but in fact his fall will be the greater. For Mark, Galilee is more than a geographical place; it is also symbolic of the mission of Jesus. The promise of a meeting in Galilee after the resurrection points to a new mission for the disciples. Despite what will happen in Gethsemane, Jesus shows that he has foreseen and already chosen his fate. It is not that Jesus wanted to suffer, but he was prepared to accept the Passion as the price to be paid in order to bring new life to the world. By plumbing the depths of human suffering and taking on himself our death, he drew its sting and gave all people the possibility of sharing in his eternal life.

Peter tries to separate himself from the other disciples and seems very sure of himself. Jesus addresses him very solemnly: Peter will deny any knowledge of Jesus. Peter refuses to accept this and becomes even more bombastic. The reference to denial three times might bear a hint of the legal procedures in the Roman Empire where suspects were asked three times whether they were Christians. The prediction of Peter's denial (*Mark* 14:30; *Matthew* 26:34; *Luke* 22:34; *John* 13:38) and the actual denial (*Mark* 14:66-72; *Matthew* 26:69-75; *Luke* 22:56-62; *John* 18:25-27) appear in all the Gospels. The picture of Peter gradually gets better as the years pass and the other Evangelists have an opportunity to reflect on his importance in the Church.

The failure of the disciples is not the most prominent part of the story. Jesus triumphs over death and over the betrayal even of his closest friends.

Reflecting

Jesus leaves to his disciples his farewell gift, which is his continuing presence in the Eucharist. We who share in the Eucharist of the Lord are called to be his intimate friends. In Mark there is a great stress on the lack of understanding shown by the disciples towards Jesus' message. They argued about who would be greatest in the Kingdom of God. Finally they all deserted Jesus. Peter, James and John could not keep awake with him in his agony. Peter's denial of Jesus

---
13 *Ibid*, pp. 112-115.

is stressed. He who was the leader of the apostles denies even knowing him. Peter had told Jesus, "Even though all the others fall away, I will not" (14:29) and even after Jesus had prophesied his threefold denial, he said even more earnestly, "Though I have to die with you, I will never deny you" (14:31). They all said the same and I am sure they believed it.

Each one of us who claims to follow Christ must examine ourselves closely. Do you betray Christ? Of course you would not dream of doing that consciously, but do you betray his message? We are called to bring the Good News about God's revelation of love in His Son to others. Are you a bearer of Good News to others by the way you live or do you turn people away from Jesus by your hypocrisy or lack of care? Are you willing to stay with Jesus when things are going well but not when it is tough to be a Christian? Mark stresses the deficiencies of the Twelve in order to point out to his own community and indeed to all readers that no follower of Christ can rest on his or her laurels, secure in his or her own goodness. Mark's own Christian community had probably experienced betrayal and apostasy during persecution. Once the persecution had died down they faced the problem of how to deal with that situation. They would have taken heart at the portrayal of the Twelve and especially of Peter. Christ came to call sinners and not the just. We cannot save ourselves; we do need God. You may lead a reasonably good life, in your own opinion, but perhaps the only reason you have not done some of the things you disapprove of in others is that you have not been tested very much. The realisation of the possibilities for sin in our lives can be shocking but it is ultimately healthy because it keeps us humble, knowing the truth about ourselves.

The betrayal of Jesus is placed firmly in the context of the Eucharist, which is the sign and instrument of unity within the community gathered round the Lord. Judas is constantly called one of the Twelve to underline the enormity of his deed. He had been a friend and disciple of Jesus, one who shared meals with him (*Mark* 14:18). Jesus was not only rejected by his opponents, he was betrayed by one of his close friends with whom he had shared his life. The name of Judas is associated with treachery but Mark wants every Christian to ask the question which all the apostles asked: "You don't mean me, do you?"(14:19). Jesus did not celebrate the Eucharist with saints but with people whose faith was extremely shaking. He was used to sharing meals with people who were a bit questionable (cf. 2:15-17). Are you the "right sort" to be sharing in the Eucharist? Do you judge the motives of other people who go to church?

Here are a few questions that might help you to ponder more deeply what God may be saying to you through the text of Scripture we have been reading. There

JESUS IS BETRAYED

are no right or wrong answers to these questions, but perhaps in pondering them you may be able to listen to the Word of God at a deeper level.

1. Peter was too sure of his own strength and he ended up denying that he knew Christ. What keeps you from denying Christ?
2. What does the Eucharist mean to you? What could you do to increase your understanding and your appreciation of this gift which Jesus left for his followers?

The story of the owner of the house

My servant brought the two men to the house and I wondered who they were. I was happy to hear that they were followers of Jesus. I knew that he was in trouble and that I might have some trouble too when I gave him and his friends hospitality. They wanted to celebrate the Passover and it is our pious duty to extend hospitality especially at this time of year so I gladly gave the upper room over to them. Jesus thanked me when he arrived. There is something about him. He has authority. It is different from the rulers of this nation or the Romans. He has a quiet authority about him as if he is in control. I still feel that even after what happened to him. I don't know what to believe about what his disciples are saying but there was definitely something about him.

Responding

At this point you might have another read of the Gospel passage in this Station. We have tried to understand it a bit more deeply and reflect on its meaning for us. There was a lot in it. We read about the Last Supper where Jesus gave himself to his friends to replace the lamb that was traditionally sacrificed to seal the bond of love between God and the people. Jesus was aware that what he was doing was establishing a new covenant or a new bond of love. However, this gift of his life took place in an atmosphere of betrayal. Jesus knew that he would be betrayed by someone very close to him. He also knew that Simon Peter would deny him and that the others would run away when he needed them. He knew that he would be left alone.

Now is the time to let go of our thinking and let our heart speak to the heart of God. Share what you are feeling with God. Nothing is off-limits. To start you off, below you will find a poetic translation of the famous hymn by St. Thomas

Aquinas, *Adoro Te Devote*, about the Eucharist. If it helps, read it slowly, put the book down and speak to God in your heart, but remember to listen also.

> *Prostrate I adore Thee, Deity unseen,*
> *Who Thy glory hidest 'neath these shadows mean;*
> *Lo, to Thee surrendered, my whole heart is bowed,*
> *Tranced as it beholds Thee, shrined within the cloud.*
>
> *Taste, and touch, and vision, to discern Thee fail;*
> *Faith, that comes by hearing, pierces through the veil.*
> *I believe whate'er the Son of God hath told;*
> *What the Truth hath spoken, that for truth I hold.*
>
> *On the Cross lay hidden but thy Deity,*
> *Here is hidden also Thy Humanity:*
> *But in both believing and confessing, Lord,*
> *Ask I what the dying thief of Thee implored.*
>
> *Thy dread wounds, like Thomas, though I cannot see,*
> *His be my confession, Lord and God, of Thee,*
> *Make my faith unfeigned ever-more increase,*
> *Give me hope unfading, love that cannot cease.*
>
> *O memorial wondrous of the Lord's own death;*
> *Living Bread, that giveth all Thy creatures breath,*
> *Grant my spirit ever by Thy life may live,*
> *To my taste Thy sweetness never-failing give.*
>
> *Pelican of mercy, Jesu, Lord and God,*[14]
> *Cleanse me, wretched sinner, in Thy Precious Blood:*
> *Blood where one drop for human-kind outpoured*
> *Might from all transgression have the world restored.*
>
> *Jesu, whom now veiled, I by faith descry,*
> *What my soul doth thirst for, do not, Lord, deny,*
> *That thy face unveiled, I at last may see,*
> *With the blissful vision blest, my God, of Thee. Amen.*

---

14 In medieval Europe there was a legend that the Pelican would feed its young with its own blood if no other food was available. The pelican became a symbol for the Passion of Christ and for the Eucharist.

Resting

There comes a time when we have no more to say or perhaps we have no words to express what is in our heart. At this time, the gentle invitation from God is to rest in the Word, which will feed us in a way that is beyond what we can see or feel. When Pope Benedict visited Britain in 2010, he spoke briefly from his heart to a large crowd of young people gathered outside Westminster Cathedral in London. During this talk he said:

> *I ask you to look into your hearts, each day, to find the source of all true love. Jesus is always there quietly waiting for us to be still with him and to hear his voice. Deep within your heart, he is calling you to spend time with him in prayer, but this kind of prayer, real prayer, requires discipline. It requires time for moments of silence every day. Often it means waiting for the Lord to speak. Even amidst the business and stress of our daily lives we need to make space for silence, because it is in silence that we find God. And [it is] in silence that we discover our true self.*[15]

How do we hear the Lord's voice in the silence of our hearts? Of course when we try to enter into silence, lots of thoughts will arise about what we must do or should be doing or what we have forgotten to do. Perhaps we will remember some offence, real or imagined, to our dignity. Whatever the thoughts that emerge, let them come and let them go. Don't try to fight them because that is changing your focus away from God to whatever particular thought you are struggling with. As long as you are alive you will have stray thoughts. They are part and parcel of our prayer. They will always be there, but they will only have the energy that you choose to give them. Do not bother with them and they will have no energy and will come and go. I realise that some thoughts are particularly juicy and are difficult to ignore. Sometimes you will be drawn away from where you want your mind and heart to be. As soon as you become aware of losing your focus, let your heart return to being in the presence of God and don't get upset with yourself. God created us and knows what we are like.

The Old Testament prophets criticised the people for going after dumb idols. The psalms said that idols had mouths but they did not speak (*Psalm* 115:5). That was a major difference to the God of Israel, the true God, who spoke especially through the prophets. In the New Testament we are told that in the beginning was the Word through whom all things came to be (*John* 1:1-2). So

---

15 Pope Benedict XVI, *Heart Speaks Unto Heart: Pope Benedict XVI in the United Kingdom - The Complete Addresses and Homilies*, (London: Darton, Longman & Todd, 2010), pp. 77-78.

God speaks to us principally through His Son, Jesus Christ. God will speak to us in silence, and this will be a word of love. We will not hear a human voice, but if we listen with faith we will understand that God is the Source of our life and that this God is very near us.

Listen now. Let all the distracting thoughts come and go. Listen with faith.

What's Next?

What is next? What is the effect of all our prayer and reflection on the Scriptures? If our prayer does not change us in some way or give us the impetus to do something positive for another person, then it is suspect. The point of prayer is not to make us feel good but to slowly shape us to become fit for the Kingdom of God which Jesus proclaimed in all his preaching and by all his miracles. At the Last Supper he said that he would not drink wine again until he drank it new in the Kingdom of God.

Jesus was betrayed in different ways by those who were close to him. In the next day or two, try to live his message faithfully. Treat other people the way you would like them to treat you.

*Christ's Agony in the Garden.
Ceramic by Adam Kossowski on the Rosary Way at Aylesford Priory, Kent,
marking the First Sorrowful Mystery.*

The Fourth Station

IN GETHSEMANE

Mark 14:32-52

Prayer

Oh God, your Son Jesus, was afraid as his passion and death approached. I too get afraid about some things that might happen in the future. Jesus ended his prayer confident that, come what may, You would be with him. Help me to believe that too and experience your presence throughout my life. Amen.

Text

There have been very many translations of the Bible throughout the centuries. The one we use in this Station is from the *New American Bible* (*NAB*). This was made specifically for the American market. It is a work of Catholic biblical scholars intended for use in public worship and first published in 1970. There have been second (1986) and third (1991) editions in which the language has been changed to make it more inclusive. In the year 2000 the New Testament and Psalms were modified again for use in the liturgy.[16]

> [32] Then they came to a place named Gethsemane, and he said to his disciples, "Sit here while I pray." [33] He took with him Peter, James, and John, and began to be troubled and distressed. [34] Then he said to them, "My soul is sorrowful even to death. Remain here and keep watch." [35] He advanced a little and fell to the ground and prayed that if it were possible the hour might pass by him; [36] he said, "Abba, Father, all things are possible to you. Take this cup away from me, but not what I will but what you will." [37] When he returned he found them asleep. He said to Peter, "Simon, are you asleep? Could you not keep watch for one hour? [38] Watch and pray that you may not undergo the test. The spirit is willing but the flesh is weak." [39] Withdrawing again, he prayed, saying the same thing. [40]

---

[16] *The New American Bible*, edited by Louis Hartman and Myles Bourke, available in various editions. The passage is taken from the *New American Bible with Revised New Testament and Revised Psalms* © 1991, 1986, 1970 Confraternity of Christian Doctrine, Washington, D.C., and used by permission of the copyright owner. All rights reserved.

JESUS IS BETRAYED

Then he returned once more and found them asleep, for they could not keep their eyes open and did not know what to answer him. [41] He returned a third time and said to them, "Are you still sleeping and taking your rest? It is enough. The hour has come. Behold, the Son of Man is to be handed over to sinners. [42] Get up, let us go. See, my betrayer is at hand." [43] Then, while he was still speaking, Judas, one of the Twelve, arrived, accompanied by a crowd with swords and clubs who had come from the chief priests, the scribes, and the elders. [44] His betrayer had arranged a signal with them, saying, "The man I shall kiss is the one; arrest him and lead him away securely." [45] He came and immediately went over to him and said, "Rabbi." And he kissed him. [46] At this they laid hands on him and arrested him. [47] One of the bystanders drew his sword, struck the high priest's servant, and cut off his ear. [48] Jesus said to them in reply, "Have you come out as against a robber, with swords and clubs, to seize me? [49] Day after day I was with you teaching in the temple area, yet you did not arrest me; but that the scriptures may be fulfilled." [50] And they all left him and fled. [51] Now a young man followed him wearing nothing but a linen cloth about his body. They seized him, [52] but he left the cloth behind and ran off naked.

Reading

Raymond Brown opens his two volume study of the Passion of the Lord immediately after the Last Supper when Jesus goes off to pray and is arrested (*Mark* 14:26-52; *Matthew* 26:30-56; *Luke* 22:39-53; *John* 18:1-11). This is, strictly speaking, where the story of the Passion begins. All four Gospels converge to a great extent in the development of the story. In all the Gospels the passion story is preceded by a build-up of a foreboding atmosphere. We have followed this build-up in the previous three Stations. Jesus goes to pray across the Kidron Valley (John) on the Mount of Olives (Synoptics) to a place called Gethsemane (Mark and Matthew). In the Prophet Zechariah, the Mount of Olives is mentioned as the place on which God's feet will rest on the day that God fights against the nations (14:4). Throughout the Gospel we have seen Jesus talking about his own approaching death with seeming calm. Therefore what happens in the garden is shocking. It seems that all the Gospel writers had in mind the scene of King David escaping from the rebellion of his son Absalom. David made his way up to the Mount of Olives weeping as he went (*2 Samuel* 15:30).

Jesus asks his disciples to wait for him while he goes to pray. Mark often uses the word "disciple" but this is the last time until after the proclamation of the resurrection. All the disciples failed Jesus and were not worthy of the name. He takes with him his three closest friends, Peter, James and John, who had accompanied him at the scene of the Transfiguration (*Mark* 9:2-8) and at the raising of Jairus' daughter (*Mark* 5:37). In the garden, according to Mark, Jesus becomes greatly distressed and troubled (14:34). This language reflects the psalms when they describe the innocent man who suffers (cf. *Psalm* 42:5, 11; 43:5). Matthew softens the portrait of Jesus somewhat, as does Luke. As well as John, Luke always presents Jesus as very much in command. However, Mark and Matthew come at it from another perspective. Now is the moment when Jesus must face the reality of sin and evil. This is the supreme test for Jesus.

Jesus wants to be alone with the Father so that he can share his feeling of dread but he does not want to be completely alone so he tells Peter, James and John that he is deeply distressed and asks them to watch with him. Jesus prays that the hour might pass him by. This is not just referring to a particular period of time but to the events in which the plan of God will come to fruition. Jesus is asking that there might be another way. In the *Letter to the Hebrews*, it is said that while he lived on earth, "he offered up prayer and entreaty, aloud and with silent tears" (5:7). Mark does not intend to tell us about the psychological state of Jesus. His interest lies in bringing his readers face to face with the scandal of the Messiah who was rejected, the Son who was killed.

In John's Gospel, the "hour" of Jesus is a very important concept and here Mark uses it to refer to the moment when Jesus will sacrifice himself for the life of the world. Mark likes to use Aramaic words and phrases now and again. These go right back to Jesus himself as that was the language he spoke. In Judaism, God was known as Father but normally this was understood in a collective sense as being the father of the people and not of an individual. Jesus uses a very intimate familiar term to speak to God, one that had not been used before, at least in the writings that have come down to us. Jesus asks that this cup be taken from him, that is, the suffering and death that is waiting for him in a few short hours. "Cup" was a very common word used in the Bible to signify great suffering (cf. *Psalm* 75:8; *Isaiah* 51:17-22; *Jeremiah* 25:15). However, even in this extreme moment, Jesus does not want to follow his own will but the will of his Father which he knows is for the salvation of the world. Jesus makes his definitive choice. The will of the Father is not a cruel and absurd destiny but is now the will of Jesus himself, who wants to be in solidarity with all those who are excluded, with sinners, even in death, and particularly in the kind of death he is facing.

JESUS IS BETRAYED

Jesus returns to his friends but finds them asleep. Concern for them along with his own prayer occupy the last moments before his arrest. The commitment that Jesus had to his disciples dominated his public ministry. He does not abandon them at this time of deep suffering for himself. He is still instructing his disciples how to act in times of difficulty. However, notice that Jesus uses Peter's own name of "Simon", that is, the name he bore before he became a disciple. What he was doing was not worthy of a disciple of Christ, and so he becomes a symbol of the failure of all the disciples to remain with Jesus at the time of his greatest need. They must watch and pray lest they enter into temptation or be put to the test. As well as the great suffering that Jesus is about to endure, the "test" refers also to the moment of crisis when human beings are asked to choose for or against God. These men had followed Christ and seen so much, but their faith was weak and there was a danger that they could fall away completely.

In verse 41 there is a mysterious expression of Jesus, after he finds his three friends asleep for the third time: "It is enough". This might mean that Judas has received the agreed price for betraying Jesus, or that the disciples have slept enough, or that Jesus has finished praying and now is in complete union with the will of the Father. It might also mean that the public ministry of Jesus has come to an end and that the final act is about to take place. Those different ways of interpreting a seemingly simple phrase give an indication that we cannot always assume that the meaning of something in the Bible is obvious. Perhaps there is a bit more to it than we might think.

In Gethsemane, Jesus was tempted to eliminate suffering from his way but he overcame this temptation. However, part of the immense suffering of Gethsemane could also have been an understanding on the part of Jesus that his struggle was not just against sinners but against Evil itself. This is a reminder of the petition of the Lord's Prayer about not putting us to the test ("Lead us not into temptation"). While Mark does not actually mention the prayer as such, he has several of the elements dotted about his Gospel. Jesus fully accepts his Father's will, not without a struggle, and he meets those who come to arrest him with great dignity. All his disciples desert him because they are frightened. Jesus was alone but nevertheless he embraced his destiny and so he brought about our salvation.

When Jesus returns from praying to his Father for the third time, he seems to have a new energy and he is ready to face whatever will be thrown at him. Some men, led by Judas, enter the garden, armed with swords and clubs, to arrest Jesus (*Mark* 14:43). Judas kisses Jesus as a sign to the crowd to arrest him, but it is also traditionally a sign of friendship. Judas has warned the band he is accompanying to arrest Jesus and hold him securely as if he was afraid that his friend might escape. A treacherous kiss is mentioned in several stories in the Old Testament and in the *Book of Proverbs* we are told: "from one who hates kisses are ominous" (27:6b). Each Gospel has its own particular perspective, but they all agree that Jesus was arrested, as well as on certain details of the scene, including the cutting off of the servant's ear (*Mark* 14:47; *Matthew* 26:51; *Luke* 22:49-50; *John* 18:10). He is the servant of the High Priest. One translator suggests that it was the earlobe that was cut off.[17] In Mark's story Jesus makes no response to this, while in the other Gospels he clearly disapproves. Jesus then complains that the way they have come to arrest him gives the impression that he is a man of violence, while the truth is that he preached openly in the Temple day after day.

At the Last Supper, Jesus had prophesied that all would have their faith shaken (*Mark* 14:27) and now all the disciples run away, accepting that the-powers-that-be have Jesus in their grasp. However the word "disciple" is not used and it has been suggested that Mark has done this on purpose as those who run away – rather than taking up their cross and following Jesus – are not worthy of the name. The young man who flees from the scene is not mentioned in the other Gospels. He is quite mysterious and there have been all sorts of guesses as to who this might be or what he might represent, but nothing can be stated with any degree of certainty. The Prophet Amos speaks of a day when even the bravest warriors will run away naked (2:16). Perhaps it is the memory of one who was actually present. The disciples had to leave everything to follow Jesus at the beginning of his public ministry (*Mark* 1:16-20). Now they have to leave everything in order to run away. Now Jesus is alone in the hands of his enemies.

Reflecting

Read again slowly the text from St. Mark's Gospel that we have been looking at in this station (14:32-52).

The foreboding atmosphere that has been building up comes to a head in this story of Jesus going with his disciples to the Mount of Olives, to a place there called Gethsemane, and we see him praying in agony to his Father. Most experts agree that Mark's Gospel, which is the shortest, was the first to be written. Matthew and Luke most probably based their versions on what Mark wrote. Each of the Evangelists has a particular approach, and Mark wants to present

---

17 Nicholas King, *The New Testament*, (Stowmarket, Suffolk: Kevin Mayhew Ltd., 2004), p. 116.

JESUS IS BETRAYED

Jesus as the Messiah, the Son of God, who calls people to follow him. Mark's community was probably experiencing great persecution, and so he points out that Jesus asked his followers to renounce themselves and take up their cross because "anyone who want to save his life will lose it but anyone who loses his life for my sake, and for the sake of the gospel, will save it" (8:34-35). Peter did not like what Jesus said, but Jesus accuses him of following human ways of thinking and not God's ways (8:33).

Some people have an impression of Jesus that has nothing to do with the portrait that the Gospel writers present. The reaction of Peter when Jesus first told his disciples what would happen to him was very human. We naturally seek life and abhor rejection, suffering and death. When we are dominated by this way of thinking we block out what we do not want to hear and so we perhaps want to eliminate suffering from the path of Christian discipleship. Jesus himself was tempted to escape suffering and this seems to have been the root of his struggle in the garden on the night before he died. He was a man who suffered like any man, but he understood that he had a unique relationship with God and he wanted other people to share in this relationship. Jesus realised that they, too, would have to struggle against evil and sin. He realised that his suffering and death was according to the will of his Father, whom he loved and who loved him. He was sent to bring life to the world but the opposition was such that Jesus understood that only by his death would liberation come to the human race from what enslaved them. This was the reason that he had been born. Nevertheless, he was afraid. From the very first time that Jesus announced his destiny he spoke with great calm, almost as if he was speaking of someone else. However, in the garden he faces his destiny up close.

Jesus has known from the first prediction of the Passion that his destiny is the will of God. In the garden he freely expresses his emotions to his Father, but finally accepts that there is no other way to bring salvation to the world except through his death.

The natural human reaction is to oppose evil with evil, force with force, violence with violence. However, we know from bitter experience that the way of retaliation leads nowhere except to a further spiral of violence. God's way is different. Jesus is called to face evil and violence with love and peace. This makes the violent even more violent, but it is the only way to break the vicious circle of hatred.

Jesus embraced suffering and death in loving obedience to his Father's will and so he pronounced the death sentence on death itself. "Jesus' fear is far more radical than the fear that everyone experiences in the face of death: it is the collision between light and darkness, between life and death itself – the critical moment of decision in human history."[18] We cannot have the glory of the resurrection without the cross. We are asked to choose. Will you commit yourself to Christ's way and fight with the invincible weapons of love and peace, or will you go the way of the world which leads you into a maze of hatred?

Jesus struggled against external evil but we must also struggle against an evil that is within. Each one of us has a dark side to our personality that we would rather not face. We become integrated, whole, when we are able to embrace our shadow, or our darker side. When we embrace our weakness by accepting it totally as part of ourselves, it can become a great strength for us. Saint Paul said, "When I am weak, then I am strong" (*2 Corinthians* 12:10). This acceptance, however, does not come about except after a great struggle, as we generally have an image of ourselves that we desperately want to be true. At some point we will come face to face with our weakness. It can be quite a shock to look within ourselves and see the lack of love and the possibilities for sin that lurk in the depths of our being. The acceptance of ourselves as we really are is the victory of truth over falsehood. If our lives are planted in truth, we will follow the way which leads to life and we will become the persons God always intended us to be.

Jesus must face his destiny alone. In the end each one of us must meet our destiny alone. No one can make our decisions for us – we make them on our own. We must stand alone before God. We can be influenced by others but no one can take our place. Each one of has a song to sing, and no one can sing it for us.

Jesus spoke to his Father as "Abba". Saint Paul also uses the same word as a way of expressing the Christian's relationship to God (*Romans* 8:15; *Galatians* 4:6). It seems clear that the use of this intimate term for God was very common among the first Christians. We can speak to God as Jesus himself did because we become sons and daughters of God in Christ.

Jesus tells his disciples in the garden to pray so that they not be put to the test. In the Old Testament, it is God who puts people to the test, but in the New Testament the understanding is a little different. God never tempts us to sin, but may allow a situation whereby we are tested. This situation teaches us a lot about ourselves. We may find out that we are not as strong in faith or morals as we thought we were, or the test may strengthen our resolve. Therefore in the *Our Father*, when we ask God not to lead us into temptation, we are asking for God's help and strength so that we do not fall.

---

[18] Pope Benedict XVI, *Jesus of Nazareth*, op. cit., pp. 155-56.

JESUS IS BETRAYED

When Jesus returns to the disciples, he finds them asleep. Something has happened in his prayer because he is now in full possession of himself and ready to face whatever will be thrown at him. There seems to be an intentional connection with the story earlier in Mark's Gospel (13:33-37) about the man going on a journey who leaves his servants in charge of his house. He may return at any time and must not find the servants asleep. It is an exhortation to also be alert for we do not know when the Lord will return. In the scene in Gethsemane, Jesus makes the story real. Jesus invites his friends to accompany him on his way of the cross: "Get up. Let us go" (14:42), but they run away. What is your reaction?

This scene of the agony in the garden teaches Christians not to be over-confident. Being faithful when times are good is somewhat easier than when difficulties came upon us.

The Word of God is something alive and active (*Hebrews* 4:12) and is intended to bring us to the fullness of life. The Word is directed towards each one of us. Therefore what might God be saying to you through this story of Jesus' agonised prayer in the garden?

The following questions are intended to help you delve a little deeper into the Word of God. There are no right or wrong answers, only your answers. Take your time and ponder them one by one before God.

1. How does it feel to see Jesus in great distress?
2. How would you have comforted Jesus?
3. Do you seek to conform your will to that of God?
4. Do you pray not to undergo the test?

The young man's story

I'm not going to tell you my name. I'm still too ashamed. I was there. I was not old enough to follow Jesus around but I did listen to him when he came to Jerusalem. What he said fascinated me. I could never understand the scribes. They made our religion sound so complicated but when Jesus spoke about God, it was all so different. He talked about the Reign of God and all we had to do was accept God's love into our hearts. He spoke of mercy not sacrifice, and treating each other with respect, forgiving each other when we do anything to offend. I thought that when I am older I will follow him just like the one they call Peter and the others.

Whenever he spoke in Jerusalem there were always people who tried to oppose him or trick him, but the people believed him and not his enemies. Jesus and his friends celebrated the Passover in a house close to my home. I had to be with my family for the meal. It's tradition, but as soon as I could I got out and someone told me they had gone to Gethsemane. I followed them there. Just as I got there a big crowd arrived. They had clubs and spears. There were Temple police with them. I hid behind a tree, and then they grabbed hold of Jesus. There was a fight but Jesus tried to calm everyone down. The crowd were dragging him away and his friends tried to rescue him but then they all ran away. One of the crowd spotted me and tried to grab me too. He took hold of the cloth I had draped around me but I struggled out of it and ran away naked. I ran and ran. I was shaking and crying. After a bit, when I thought everyone had gone, I went back to look for my clothes. I found the cloth on the ground. It was all dirty but better than running home naked.

I wanted to follow him but I ran away. It's too late now ... but maybe not.

Responding

Have another read of the story of Jesus in Gethsemane (*Mark* 14:32-52). We have read the Word of God carefully and thought about it from various angles, but prayer really begins when our heart becomes involved in the relationship with God. It is time now to put the book down and speak to God from your heart. Maybe you want to argue with God or express how you feel about what happened to Jesus. Whatever it is, it can become prayer if you share it with God.

To get you going you might want to use the words of *Psalm* 109. Say them slowly and then let your heart speak to the heart of God:

> [2] O God, whom I praise, do not be silent, for wicked and treacherous mouths attack me. They speak against me with lying tongues;
>
> [3] with hateful words they surround me, attacking me without cause.
>
> [4] In return for my love they slander me, even though I prayed for them.
>
> [5] They repay me evil for good, hatred for my love.

Resting

The reason for much of the chatter that goes on inside us and which comes to the fore when we try to be silent is that the selfish bit of us, the part that is out to make sure we get what we think we need, keeps up a constant commentary on other people, events or things. Often we are unaware of this background noise, but when we try to be silent the volume seems to be turned up.

Sometimes the selfishness that is part of every human being is called the 'false self'.[19] We allow the false self to dominate when we seek happiness in the wrong places. God desires us to have life and have it to the full (cf. *John* 10:10) but we think that we can grasp this fullness of life by our own efforts. This has been the downfall of human beings since the beginning of time. In *Genesis*, the first book of the Bible, we can read the story of the tree of the knowledge of good and evil (*Genesis* 2:15-17). The first man and woman were given all the other trees to eat from except that one. Which one did they eat from? You guessed correctly – the forbidden fruit! So something inside us seems to grab hold of what we hope will bring life but which instead brings death.

Everybody wants to be happy; God wants us to be happy. However, we tend to have different views of how to get there. In one of the stories about King Solomon, God offers him whatever he wants (*1 Kings* 3:5-12). What will he choose – wealth, victory over his enemies, fame? What would you choose? How do you fancy winning the lottery, or perhaps winning one of the many talent contests on the television and so achieving fame? Solomon chose wisdom, a heart capable of discerning between good and evil. In the story we are told that God was pleased with Solomon's choice. If we have wisdom, we will know how to handle a long or a short life, good health or bad health, poverty or plenty, fame or obscurity, power or the lack of it. If we do not have wisdom, the ups and downs of life can embitter us.

The false self looks for happiness in ways that can never satisfy. Often the thoughts that pop into our heads when we are trying to be silent come from this false part of us. The best way to deal with these thoughts is not to resist them, not to try to retain them, not to react to them, but simply to seek to return to the gentle silence of listening to the still, small voice of God who alone can lead us to a happiness that will fully and finally satisfy us.

---

[19] For some more information on the 'false self' see the first six chapters of Thomas Keating, *Invitation To Love: The Way of Christian Contemplation*, (Rockport, Massachusetts & Shaftesbury, Dorset: Element Books, 1992). A simple explanation of the 'false self' can be found in Elizabeth Smith and Joseph Chalmers, *A Deeper Love: An Introduction to Centering Prayer*, (London & New York: Continuum, 1999), pp. 83-97.

Take some time now to be silent in God's presence. We have read the Word of God, thought about it, prayed about it. Now seek the Source of all that is. Be still and know that God is with you.

What's Next?

Perhaps you cannot comfort Jesus but you can comfort someone else. Try to bring comfort to someone today.

"Their verdict was unanimous: Jesus deserved to die."
(Mark 14:64)

The Fifth Station

BEFORE THE SANHEDRIN

Mark 14:53-65

Jesus was accused that he had claimed to destroy the Temple made by human hands and in three days rebuild another, not made with human hands.

Prayer

O God, you sent your Son into the world to bring us life and we treated him with scorn. So many people are despised and maltreated in our world. Keep them in your care. Touch the hearts of those who treat others with cruelty that they may be converted. Through Christ Our Lord. Amen.

Text

The text below is taken from the *New Jerusalem Bible*, which is a translation by Catholic scholars dating from 1985.[20] It is a complete revision of the *Jerusalem Bible*, published in 1966. It was intended primarily as a study Bible and so accuracy of translation was the prime consideration. It has become the most widely-used Catholic Bible outside the U.S.A. It has also been widely used for liturgical purposes, and so care has been taken to make the language fresh and lively but also dignified.

Read what happens in this part of the story in order to get an idea of the overall sense and to take in the details.

> [53] They led Jesus off to the high priest; and all the chief priests and the elders and the scribes assembled there. [54] Peter had followed him at a distance, right into the high priest's palace, and was sitting with the attendants warming himself at the fire. [55] The chief priests and the whole Sanhedrin were looking for evidence against Jesus in order to have him executed. But they could not find any. [56] Several, indeed, brought false witness against him, but

---

[20] *The New Jerusalem Bible*, edited by Henry Wansbrough, O.S.B., (London: Darton, Longman & Todd, 1985) © Darton, Longman & Todd Ltd. and Doubleday & Company Ltd. (a division of Random House); used with permission.

their evidence was conflicting. ⁵⁷ Some stood up and submitted this false evidence against him, ⁵⁸ 'We heard him say, "I am going to destroy this Temple made by human hands, and in three days build another, not made by human hands."' ⁵⁹ But even on this point their evidence was conflicting. ⁶⁰ The high priest then rose before the whole assembly and put this question to Jesus, 'Have you no answer to that? What is this evidence these men are bringing against you?' ⁶¹ But he was silent and made no answer at all. The high priest put a second question to him saying, 'Are you the Christ, the Son of the Blessed One?' ⁶² 'I am,' said Jesus, 'and you will see the Son of man seated at the right hand of the Power and coming with the clouds of heaven.' ⁶³ The high priest tore his robes and said, 'What need of witnesses have we now? ⁶⁴ You heard the blasphemy. What is your finding?' Their verdict was unanimous: he deserved to die. ⁶⁵ Some of them started spitting at his face, hitting him and saying, 'Play the prophet!' And the attendants struck him too.

Now let us see a little of what lies behind the story.

Reading

Jesus is then led off to the high priest, whom Mark does not name. Matthew (26:3) and John (11:49; 18:13, 24) identify him as Caiaphas, who was high priest from 18 to 36 or 37 A.D. He was removed from office shortly after Pontius Pilate was dismissed as Procurator or Governor in 36 A.D. All the high priests, presumably referring to those who had held the role previously, plus the scribes and elders gather together. A little further on, we are told that this is the Sanhedrin, which was a group of religious leaders and other prominent citizens within Judaism that had responsibility in religious and some secular matters under the Roman Procurator, who appointed the High Priest. The Sanhedrin was not strictly speaking a court but dealt with all sorts of matters as the group saw fit. It is not really known how many were members of this group or where they normally met at the time of Jesus. In this section of the story of the Passion, they come together in the house of the high priest. It is also impossible to decide whether the "trial" of Jesus was a fair one as we do not know for certain what rules, if any, the Sanhedrin followed, and the Gospel accounts are not exactly phrased as modern law reports would be. It might have been a cross examination before deciding to hand Jesus over to the Roman authorities.[21] The Gospels are not intended to be a chronicle of what exactly happened; they bear a message of Good News from God and they interpret the death of Jesus in terms of the biblical prophecies.

All the Gospels agree, however, with the basic idea that the Sanhedrin authorities were involved in seizing Jesus and handing him over to the Romans for execution. The Gospels differ on the degree of guilt to be borne by this group and on how representative they were of the people as a whole. The Gospel writers were, of course, profoundly affected by the situation that existed as they were writing. A very bitter dispute arose between Jews who rejected Jesus and those who accepted him as the Messiah. The latter group, after some time, welcomed non-Jews into their community, and this widened the split even further. This dispute colours the story of the Passion.

Peter is the only disciple who has the courage to follow Jesus right into the courtyard of the high priest's house. Mark shows the chief priests and the scribes as being determined on the death of Jesus. They were "looking for evidence against Jesus in order to have him executed" (14:55). They had made up their minds that Jesus had to die. They were willing to give Judas money in order to bring this about with the least trouble possible (14:1-2, 10-11). They seek testimony against Jesus, but when this proves false or inconsistent they condemn him for blasphemy on the basis of his own words. In Raymond Brown's opinion, no one in authority gives Jesus just treatment.[22] However, Jesus did not court popularity and he made known his criticisms of the established forms of religion of his day. He would not have been a comfortable figure for those who were sure of their own righteousness. Jesus was not trying to establish himself as a particularly liberal rabbi; he was going very far beyond this. He took upon himself authority that belonged to God.

Jesus remains silent in the face of the false testimony, although there are indications in the rest of the Gospel that he did indeed prophesy an end to the Temple in Jerusalem. Pope Benedict, in his book on the experience of Jesus during Holy Week, says that Jesus loved the Temple as it belonged to the Father, but he understood that its time was over and that something new was to come, which was linked to his death and resurrection.[23] When the high priest solemnly asks him if he is the Christ, the Son of the Blessed One (a Jewish way of referring to God), he breaks his silence: "I am," said Jesus, "and you will see

---

21 Pope Benedict XVI, *Jesus of Nazareth, op. cit.*, pp. 175-76.
22 Brown, *op. cit.*, Vol. I, p. 387.
23 Pope Benedict XVI, *Jesus of Nazareth, op. cit.*, p. 35.

the Son of Man seated at the right hand of the Power and coming with the clouds of heaven" (*Mark* 14:62). This is what Mark wants to focus on. The trial scene is the climax of the portrait of Jesus that Mark has been painting throughout his whole Gospel. Jesus is the Messiah, the Son of God and the Son of Man. As the cross looms over the scene, Mark intends us to finally grasp what kind of messiah Jesus is. Now that the three titles used of Jesus throughout the Gospel are tied to his suffering and death, he is free to affirm them clearly: "I am". In his answer Jesus is quoting two Old Testament passages: *Daniel* 7:13 and *Psalm* 110:1. With this answer Jesus is affirming what the whole Gospel was written to proclaim.

The first words of Mark's Gospel are: "The beginning of the Good News about Jesus Christ, the Son of God" (1:1). In earlier parts of the Gospel, Jesus has wanted his identity to remain a secret (3:11-12) probably because the people could easily have misunderstood what the titles meant, thinking that he was to be a warrior king. However, now is the moment to speak clearly. Jesus spoke out and his answer led directly to his death as he surely must have known it would. The answer is enough and the whole body declares that Jesus must die. They understood that he was arrogantly claiming for himself what belongs to God and so was insulting God. Brown points out: "Thus, despite minor variations the four evangelists, writing in different places in different decades between 60 to 100, to different Christian audiences, give almost the same picture of the charge of blasphemy against Jesus."[24] All the people who were gathered at the Sanhedrin insulted and assaulted the condemned man (*Mark* 14:64-65). It seems that the description of this treatment was intended to remind the readers of the Suffering Servant of the Lord in the Prophet Isaiah (*Isaiah* 50:6-7). This figure became very important for the early Christians in their explanation of why Jesus had suffered and died.

The accounts of Matthew and Mark are very similar. Luke, while following the same basic story line, has his own particular emphasis. The Sanhedrin kept trying to find testimony against Jesus and it must have been a very frustrating business as it seems that one witness after another proved to be inadequate since they did not agree and Jewish law demanded verification. The traditional Jewish punishment for blasphemy was to be stoned to death (*Leviticus* 24:16a). It is not clear whether the Sanhedrin had the power to condemn someone to death but needed the Roman Governor's agreement, or whether they could only present a prisoner to him for trial.

---

24 Brown, *op. cit.*, Vol. I, p. 527.

Reflecting

Read again the text from Mark's Gospel about Jesus before the Sanhedrin (14:53-65). What might God be saying to you? Do you think Mark told this story to elicit sympathy for Jesus or perhaps there is more to it?

Raymond Brown sums up the opposition to Jesus in this way:

> *The Gospel portrait implies that Jesus would be found guilty by the self-conscious religious majority of any age and background. More than likely, however, were Jesus to appear in our time (with his challenge rephrased in terms of contemporary religious stances) and be arrested and tried again, most of those finding him guilty would identify themselves as Christians and think they were rejecting an impostor – someone who claimed to be Jesus but did not fit into their conception of who Jesus Christ was and how he ought to act.*[25]

To think that way is a little bit scary. Do I follow Jesus Christ, or my own construction of what I think he should be like? Peter followed Jesus when he was arrested but at a distance (*Mark* 14:54). How many of us would prefer to follow Jesus at a distance? We might admire him and perhaps pray now and again, but we really do not want him to come too close because instinctively we realise that he might ask something of us that will be uncomfortable.

Jesus certainly challenged his contemporaries to think about God and about their faith in different ways. Some responded with great enthusiasm, but others with profound anger because his views were challenging what they understood as essential. His parables suggested that God was different from what they had always thought. Jesus opened up new possibilities; some found them exciting while others thought of them as dangerous.

I am going to pose some questions now. Pondering them is intended not to make you feel guilty but to draw you more profoundly into the Word of God. I suggest that you take your time with them and seek to respond to them in the presence of God.

1. Where would you put yourself amongst all the characters in this story? Why?
2. Why was the Sanhedrin looking for evidence against Jesus on which they could pass the death sentence?

---

[25] Brown, *op. cit.*, Vol. I, p. 393.

BEFORE THE SANHEDRIN

3. If you had been one of the Jewish rulers, under the domination of the Romans, at the time of Jesus, what would you have done about him?
4. The response of Jesus to the high priest settled the matter. Who do you think Jesus is?

Peter's story

It was all a blur. We were in the garden with him and I'm afraid we fell asleep. Then he came to wake us up and all of a sudden there was a crowd of people led by Judas. I never trusted him but I accepted him because Jesus had called him just as he called me. They wanted to arrest Jesus; everyone started pushing and shoving and someone started waving a sword about. I think somebody got hurt. I know that is not what Jesus wanted but it's difficult to understand him sometimes. In the end we all ran off and they grabbed Jesus and led him away.

I didn't run very far; I hid behind one of the trees and then followed the crowd. They were pushing and pulling at Jesus; he seemed very calm. I wasn't calm but when the crowd arrived at the house, I slipped in to the courtyard and made a bee-line for the fire. It was a cold night. There were so many people around no one noticed me at first. I didn't know whose house it was, but listening to the others who were standing around the fire I soon learned. It was the house of the high priest! It was really fancy. There was a lot of coming and going and it seems that the whole of the Sanhedrin was coming together. I was quite hopeful that everything would turn out fine because surely our religious leaders would see who Jesus is. He is the messiah, sent by God, whom our people have awaited for centuries. I couldn't believe it when I heard that they had condemned Jesus to death. Lots of shouting came from inside the house where they were questioning Jesus. I think they were hurting him. He only tried to help people and give them hope. You know what happened then. He had prophesied all of this but I didn't listen.

Responding

Read the story of Jesus before the Sanhedrin again. We have thought about it and tried to penetrate beyond the surface meaning, asking what God is saying to us in this crucial time of Jesus' life. The point of reflecting on the Word of

God is not that we will increase our knowledge about Jesus and what happened to him, but to enter more deeply into the mystery of God's offer of salvation to humanity. "Scripture can only be understood if it is lived."[26] Let us seek to penetrate the scene in St. Mark's Gospel not by thinking about it now or studying it, but by responding to God from our hearts. What do our hearts want to say to God? Our response to the Word of God can be anything at all. In this dialogue with God we are led to a more profound relationship with the One who seeks to share the divine life with all people.

Spend as long as you like, speaking to God from your heart. To get you going, perhaps the following prayer might help:

> *Lord Jesus, your passion is the story of humanity:*
> *That story where the good are humiliated,*
> *The meek attacked,*
> *The honest are trampled.*
> *Who will be the victor?*
> *Who will have the last word?*
> *Lord Jesus,*
> *We believe that you are the last word:*
> *In You the good have already won the victory;*
> *In You, the meek have already triumphed;*
> *In You the pure of heart shine like stars in the night.*
> *The road does not end with the cross*
> *But goes beyond it*
> *To the Kingdom of Life*
> *To the explosion of Joy that no one can ever take from us.*[27]

Resting

Now is the moment to let go of your thoughts and words; now is the moment simply to rest in the Word of God. However pleasant that sounds, it is not always quite so easy. Silence can be very healing, but it can also feel like a battle because of all the thoughts that come crowding into our minds when we begin to quieten down. These thoughts, often coming from our false self, that part of us that seeks happiness in the wrong ways and the wrongs places, can exhaust us if we try to fight them, or can turn our prayer into a daydream if we give-in to them.

26　Pope Benedict XVI, *Verbum Domini – Post-Synodal Exhortation On The Word Of God* (2010), §47.
27　The prayer is my translation and adaptation of one written by Monsignor (now Cardinal) Angelo Comastri for the Stations of the Cross on Good Friday evening at the Coliseum, Rome, in 2006.

People were always taught to fight against distractions in prayer which lead the mind away from God. However, when you fight against distractions, you change your focus away from God to whatever it is you are trying to fight. There are many methods suggested nowadays to help people in their prayer. The Liturgy of the Church is the greatest prayer because it shares in the prayer of Christ to the Father in the Holy Spirit. To get the most out of the Liturgy we have to bring something to it, and what we bring to it is our own personal relationship with God that is fed by the Liturgy, by the Word of God, and by reading helpful books. One of the most traditional ways to grow in one's relationship with God is the practice of *Lectio Divina* or prayerful pondering of the Scriptures. This is the method that we have employed in the present book where we read the Word of God, reflect on it, respond to what God is saying to us, rest in God's Word, and then move outwards into daily life.

However, when we try to rest in God's Word without the prop of our own words or thoughts, we can find that we very easily become distracted. If we are distracted when we are reading or thinking, we simply return to the book we were reading or to whatever it was we were pondering; but what do we do when we become distracted as we try to be silent in the presence of God? All sorts of different methods of prayer have been suggested to help us respond to this movement towards silence in which we can become aware of God's presence. In the 1960s many young people followed the "hippy trail", apparently searching for a deeper experience of God. They did not always find the answer they were looking for. However, this phenomenon encouraged many Christians to seek within their own traditions ways that would lead to this more profound relationship with God. In the Christian tradition we have very many great mystics who have explored the dark ways of faith and reported back to us, often in the form of poetry.

The word "mystic" has a very wide meaning in popular culture where it can be reduced to someone who attempts to foretell who will win the lottery or a person who purports to tell the future by reading palms or gazing into a crystal ball. A mystic in the Christian sense is one in whom the mystery of Christ is being fulfilled as much as that can be the case on this side of the grave. Mystics look like anyone else but they are in union with God even though they may not appreciate that themselves. This is the gift of God, but also requires a response from the human being. In prayer we seek to open our hearts to God in order that God may transform us from within. There are different ways of prayer, but we must always remember the warning of Jesus not "to babble as the pagans do for they think that by using many words they will make themselves heard"

(*Matthew* 6:7). Silence is an important part of prayer and grows as we grow in intimacy with the Lord, just as it does in any close relationship. When we are very comfortable with someone, we can be silent in that person's presence without worrying how to keep the conversation going.

Let us seek now to appreciate the presence of God in silence. I suggest that you spend about fifteen minutes in this silence. Whenever you become aware that you are caught up with your own thoughts, simply return your heart to God who loves you beyond anything you could possibly imagine.

What's Next?

Having pondered the piece of Scripture where Jesus is condemned in the Sanhedrin, and spent time becoming aware of the presence of God in you and with you, now is the time to go back to your daily tasks. The people who struck Jesus and spat on him were obviously not aware of who he was. God is present in each human being. Try to treat each person you meet today with consideration.

'Peter remembered the word, how Jesus had told him,
"Before the cock crows twice, three times you will deny me."
And he thought of it and wept.'
(Mark 14:71-72)

The Sixth Station

PETER DENIES JESUS

Mark 14:66-72

Prayer

Lord, you chose Peter to follow you. He lived with you, shared your life, and yet he denied even knowing you. Let me be aware of the possibilities for betrayal that are within me so that I may depend on your grace and not on my own strength.

Text

This reading comes from a very modern translation of the New Testament by a Jesuit scholar, Nicholas King.[28] His aim is to keep as close as possible to the original Greek. Mark uses the historic present tense a lot, that is, the present tense in a past situation. This tends to make the story very vivid, but Mark was not always very grammatical and King resists the temptation to "tidy up" the text. He wants to help the reader have a similar experience that the original reader or listener to the Gospel story might have had. There are no verse numbers in this translation as that is a later invention. Punctuation was also not part of the original text, and where a translator chooses to put commas and full stops can radically alter a text. The translator of this text says that he will be happy if readers check his version with a more familiar translation. King is aware that some readers may find his translation jarring at times as he has tried to preserve the "feel" of the original Greek text. See what you think of it. Perhaps you will want to check something against another more familiar translation.

Read the text now to fix in your mind what is actually happening in the story.

> And Peter was still below in the courtyard. And there comes a single little slave girl of the High Priest. And seeing Peter warming himself she had a good look at him and says, "You were also with the Nazarene, (that) Jesus." And he denied it saying, "I neither know nor understand what you are saying." And he went out into

---

[28] *The New Testament, freshly translated by Nicholas King*, (Stowmarket, Suffolk: Kevin Mayhew Ltd., 2004), reproduced with permission.

PETER DENIES JESUS

the forecourt. And the little slave girl saw him and began again to say to the bystanders, "This (fellow) is from that lot." And he again denied (it). And again after a little the bystanders started to say to Peter, "You must certainly be (one) of them: you're a Galilean." And he began to curse and swear, "I don't know this fellow you're talking about." And immediately for the second time a cock crowed. And Peter remembered the word, how Jesus had told him, "Before the cock crows twice, three times you will deny me." And he thought of it and wept.

Reading

Before Jesus is taken off to Pilate, all the Gospels give us the scene of Peter's denial of Jesus. They already recounted the fact that Jesus had predicted this failure. This story seems to provide evidence of the truth of the Gospels, as they admit openly that the head of the apostles had failed so spectacularly. It would also have spoken very powerfully to those early Christians who suffered cruelly rather than deny their faith. It also gave hope to those who were not quite so brave and who did deny Christ. If Peter could be forgiven, then so could they.

There is a glaring contrast between Jesus, who has just openly admitted who he is, and Peter who denies being a follower. Jesus was insulted for being a false prophet, and now we see his prophecy about Peter's denial coming true. In the previous scene we had left Peter warming himself by the fire with the guards. A strange word was used for fire. It usually meant "light" and so we have the underlying idea of Peter following Jesus from a distance, still being attracted by the light but also feeling an attraction to the darkness. One of the servant girls recognises him as a disciple of Jesus; all the Gospels start off the story with this young woman. The words of the servant girl are very similar to the question that was posed to people suspected of being Christians in later persecutions, and so they would no doubt remind Mark's community of their own experience. Peter denies knowing Jesus or understanding what she is saying and moves away into the forecourt, hoping to escape the question but not willing to leave Jesus just yet.

There is a bit of dispute whether the original says that the cock crowed at this point. In some Bibles, including the translation we are using for this Station, it does not mention the noisy cock. I have read that cocks often crow around midnight and then about each hour after that until about 3 a.m., although in my limited experience they crow whenever they think you are drifting off to sleep again. However, the slave girl is not convinced by Peter's denials and either follows him to pursue her case or repeats her accusation at a later time that he is indeed one of the friends of Jesus. Each of the other Gospels names a different accuser at this point. Peter denies the accusation again. However, still Peter does not run away.

Then a little later those who are standing around join in and accuse Peter of being one of the group which was with Jesus because his Galilean accent gives him away. Peter then begins to curse and swear, denying that he had ever met Jesus. The cock lets out a second crow and Peter suddenly remembers the words of Jesus. He then dissolves into tears at the realisation of what he has done. Just at the moment that Jesus is being mocked as a bogus prophet, his words to Peter come true.

Reflecting

Peter followed at a distance until he was forced into a corner and he denied even knowing Jesus. For any follower of Christ, the time will inevitably come when we are asked to choose whether we are going to place ourselves with Christ or deny him.

There were several persecutions of Christians by Roman Emperors. One of the most notorious is Nero. He arrested some well-known Christians, some of whom informed on other Christians. The punishments that were inflicted for being a follower of Jesus were horrendous: torn to pieces by dogs, crucified, or set alight to be living torches. After the persecutions had died down, how could the betrayers and the families of those who had been so cruelly executed be reconciled? The example of Peter and Jesus would have provided hope that forgiveness was possible or would have encouraged those who had suffered to be reconciled with their fellow Christians.

Mark intends his readers and hearers to ask themselves what they would do if they were put in the same position as Peter. Very many Christians throughout the centuries have been threatened with death for their faith. Around Mark's time people were often asked to deny Jesus publicly, curse him, or be killed, so this story would have been very real.

In many parts of the world Christians are persecuted simply for following Jesus. The age of the martyrs is not over. The Twentieth Century was one of great persecution for Christian believers in many parts of the world. In some places the persecution involves the loss of life while in others it is confined to ridicule.

PETER DENIES JESUS

Following Jesus is not always comforting and comfortable. There is no shame to be afraid and even if we go to the extent of denying Jesus in some way, we can take comfort in the fact that Peter has been there before us. However, as soon as he became aware of what he had done, he repented.

It might seem, if you believed everything you heard on the TV or radio or everything you read in the papers, that no one with a pinch of intelligence goes to church any more. Without doubt there is a certain powerful lobby within the media that would like to give the impression that no intelligent person today can possibly believe in God as religion has been completely debunked by science. As well as the existence of God, Christian morality is attacked at every turn as not only outmoded but in fact as anti-human. The fact that we oppose abortion is set up as being anti-woman; the Christian anti-euthanasia stance is criticised as being cruel to those who are suffering.

Richard Dawkins' famous book *The God Delusion* made a big splash when it was first published, and this was accepted by some as the ultimate proof that there is no god. However, Dawkins' book was not a dry text of philosophy; there is burning passion behind it. For Dawkins, not only should religion be confined to what consenting adults do in private, it should be extirpated from the face of the earth because, according to him, it is more pernicious than the smallpox virus. The central argument of Dawkins' book is his chapter on "Why there is almost certainly no God". Dawkins claims that the god of the Bible is an "evil monster" and that religion is one of the world's great evils. Therefore, to bring children up in an atmosphere of faith is a form of child abuse. Also according to him, science has virtually proved that God does not exist and therefore only credulous cretins could persist in their mediaeval beliefs and practices. The fact that these two statements fly in the face of a mountain of evidence does not seem to matter, which is a bit strange for a man of science.[29]

People of faith can have a hard time in daily life and it can be tempting in certain situations to pretend that we are not of their number. Peter denied knowing Jesus; we can be tempted also, and it would be foolish to presume that we would never do what Peter did. Given the right amount of pressure, who knows what we might do? When Jesus prophesied that Peter would deny him, the leader of the disciples rejected it strongly (*Mark* 14:26-31). Peter was too sure of himself. Do not fall into the same trap. The only way to remain faithful in times of crisis is to depend on the Lord and to stay close to him.

---

29 There has been a mountain of books and articles written to defend religion against these attacks. One of the best I have read is by David Bentley Hart, *Atheist Delusions: The Christian Revolution and its Fashionable Enemies*, (New Haven & London: Yale University Press, 2009).

Prayer is the way that we remain in contact with Jesus. What we are doing in this book is trying to pray our way through the story of Christ's passion, death and resurrection. We read the Word of God which is given to us for our salvation and we try to listen carefully to what God might be saying to us. We seek to respond to God's Word from our hearts but then we allow God time to transform our hearts as we rest in silence.

Now I have some questions that hopefully will bring the story of Peter's denial of Jesus closer to home.

1. What would tempt you to deny Jesus?
2. Why do you think this story was told as part of the Passion?
3. How will you remain faithful to Christ?

The little slave girl's story

Everybody was so busy. There were lots and lots of guests and they all wanted feeding. Cook was in a bad mood so I was extra careful not to spill anything. I didn't want to get on her bad side. My job was to carry in some of the things for the guests. It wasn't a dinner or anything. There were a lot of men there with the High Priest. I have belonged to him since I was born because my mother was his slave too. I've never spoken to him and he has never spoken to me. Cook is the one that talks to me, or shouts at me I should say.

It was late and we had all been running about for hours. We had just been about to lie down for the night when a shout went up and we were all roused. I was frightened at first but then I saw that it was just one of their meetings. Only this time it was a bit different because that man Jesus was there and they dragged him into the house. I don't know what he's supposed to have done but they were all very angry. I saw him a few days ago in the city when I was out helping carry the provisions home.

All the servants and soldiers were gathered round the fire and I saw this man that I thought I had seen before. I went off to finish my work and then came back for another look. Then it hit me: I saw him with Jesus and so I said that. I thought he should be with Jesus to help him now. Anyway, this man said he didn't know what I was talking about. He was very upset and I thought he was going to hit me. So I told the porter that the man was one of the group that had been with Jesus. I probably told some other people. I am sorry I did

PETER DENIES JESUS

that now because soon it got round everybody and a couple of others said to the man that he was a liar and that he was a bad man like Jesus. Well, I am used to hearing the men swear but this man was really angry and then he started to cry. I've never seen a man cry before. I'll never forget that.

Some of the stories that are going round now are fantastic. They say that the man is the one who is the leader and is not afraid any more.

Responding

Now is the moment to speak to God from the depth of your heart. Perhaps you want to ask for help to be faithful given all the modern temptations or perhaps you want to express your own worry. Maybe you want to pray for those who are persecuted or for those who persecute others because of their faith. Learn from Peter's mistakes; do not be too sure of your own ability to be strong in time of temptation. Lean on the strong pillar of prayer. Ask God to help you "to always have your answer ready to people who ask you for the reason of the hope that you have" (*1 Peter* 3:15). The *First Letter of Peter* continues: "Give your answer with courtesy and respect and with a clear conscience, so that those who slander you when you are living a good life in Christ may be proved wrong in the accusations they bring. If it is the will of God that you should suffer, it is better to suffer for doing right than for doing wrong." (*1 Peter* 3:16-17).

Tell God now what is in your heart.

Resting

In Matthew's Gospel, Jesus gives a short teaching on prayer (6:5-15). The prayer of his disciples is to be a sincere personal communication with God. We do not need to babble as the pagans do because our Father knows what we need even before we ask. Jesus tells us to go into our "inner room, shut the door and pray to the Father there". In Jesus' day everyone certainly did not have his or her private room, so he was advising people to go off to some place where they could be alone with God. He often did that, according to the Gospels. There was one occasion when he had been busy all day teaching people and healing the sick in Capernaum, then very early in the morning, long before the dawn, he got up and went away to a deserted place so he could pray. Obviously he did not disturb anyone because when the disciples woke up they went out to search for him (*Mark* 1:21-39). Then we have also read not long ago that Jesus went off to pray on his own in the garden of Gethsemane, only this time he wanted some of his disciples to be quite near, but they fell asleep.

If you live in a city or any busy place, it is not always easy to find a deserted area where you can be alone to pray. Life also tends to be frenetic nowadays; the more "labour-saving" gadgets you have, the busier you can be. There are places of retreat, and little chapels here and there where silence reigns, and these places are to be treasured, but if you are not near one of these you could try to create your own little deserted place. The "inner room" might be your own inner depths. The Carmelite St. Teresa of Jesus presented a wonderful image of the inner depths or the soul of the human person as a beautiful castle with many dwelling places.[30] Teresa tells us that a great many people stay outside this castle and have no care about going inside. They have no idea about the beauty that lies within. The door into this castle is prayer and reflection.[31]

Life has often been pictured as a journey, and St. Teresa writes about the journey to the centre of the castle where God dwells. One passes through many different kinds of dwelling places, each with its own beauty, but the important thing is to journey onwards to the centre. Without a commitment to the relationship with God, one would get very easily distracted by all the interesting things to be found on this journey.

Our modern societies are littered with broken relationships. What makes one relationship successful and another one founder on some hidden rock? I am not a relationship counsellor and I am sure that there are all sorts of indications that might be given by such an expert. I am interested here in the relationship with God. Each relationship with God is, of course, unique, but the saints can give us some indications as to how to build a strong bond with God. Saint Teresa is very encouraging to those who have entered the interior castle, but she does point out the dangers on the way to the centre. We can easily become so preoccupied with work, or pleasure, or whatever, that we forget the journey.

'Contemplation' is all the rage nowadays among certain people. We must be careful that in all we do we are seeking only the will of God, and that our prayer does not become a subtle way of self-seeking. We can use anything to build up our own little kingdom, even prayer. Contemplation has been defined in many ways. It is a completely free gift from God which flowers in a loving, intimate knowledge of God. It is not a technique that we can learn and practice at will. God is not like the hot water tap.

---

30 St. Teresa of Jesus (of Avila), 'The Interior Castle', in *The Collected Works of St. Teresa of Avila*, Volume Two, translated by Otilio Rodriguez & Kieran Kavanaugh, (Washington, D.C.: ICS Publications, 1980).
31 *Interior Castle*, I, 5-7.

It is good to have a regular practice of prayer that will open us to God's presence and action in our lives. Vocal prayer is good, but we need to also develop a way of listening to God. What can we expect to hear when we spend time daily listening to God? It is possible that some word or phrase will pop into your mind and remain there after your time of prayer, but I think silent prayer is particularly the time when we give God the space to tune us into the 'divine wavelength'. Therefore, the fruit of our prayer is not during the prayer itself but outside. If we are 'tuned in' to God, we will begin to pick up God's gentle voice in the neighbour who needs some help, or in the situation to which we feel called to respond in some way. Perhaps we might feel the urge to go and visit someone we have not seen for a while. There are so many ways in which the voice of God can come to us, but often we are deaf to this voice.

Remember the false self, which I first referred to in the Fourth Station. This is like wearing earphones through which loud music is booming. How can you expect to hear the still, small voice of God in everyday life if your ears are filled with the latest music sensation? Therefore to experience the "secret and peaceful and loving inflow of God"[32] of course we must have a regular practice of prayer, but at the same time we must seek to dismantle the false self. The first step is to become aware of its influence in our lives. If you think you do not have a false self or that you got rid of it a long time ago, beware and think again.

I suggest that you find a place that is as quiet as you can make it, then enter into the interior castle that is your own self. Be aware that God lives at the very centre of your being. In silence, consent to God's presence with you and to whatever God is doing within you. Remember that God loves you, and that the divine action within you is to make you able to receive and appreciate a joy that "no eye has seen, no ear has heard, nor has the human heart conceived" (*1 Corinthians* 2:9). When thoughts come, as come they will, let them come and let them go.

What's Next?

The fruit of prayer has to be seen in right action. We have been reflecting on the Scripture text telling the story of Peter's denial of Jesus. He bitterly regretted this, but he obviously learned from it and he became the leader of the Christian community. We have all done things we regret. Try to learn from your own past mistakes and sins. Today try in some small way to put one of these right, or to make sure that you will not do the same thing again.

---

32 'The Dark Night' 1.10.6, in *The Collected Works of St. John of the Cross, op. cit.*

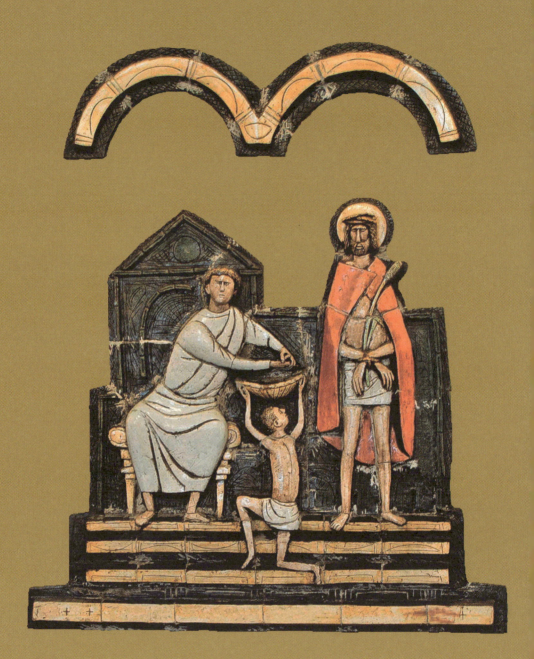

Jesus is condemned to death.
First Station in the Relic Chapel at Aylesford Priory.
Ceramic by Adam Kossowski.

The Seventh Station

PILATE CONDEMNS JESUS

Mark 15:1-15

Prayer

Compassionate God, your response to the mess human beings had made of your creation was to choose a people from whom would come the saviour. Yet when he came, he was condemned to die as a criminal. As I follow this part of Jesus' Passion, help me to be aware of the times I may condemn others without knowing the story. Pilate was swayed by the crowd and by his own interests. Help me to be aware of what influences me to make my decisions. I ask this through Christ Our Lord. Amen.

Text

The translation of our text of Scripture comes from the *New King James Version* (*NKJV*).[33] This is a revision of an ancient version compiled in England in 1611. The King referred to is James VI of Scotland (1567-1625) who took over the English throne as well in 1603 and in England is known as James I. This has been the most influential Bible translation in the English language. It was possibly the most widely read and best-known book ever published in English. While loving the language used, many felt that it had become rather old fashioned and proposed a more modern English translation, at the same time trying to preserve something of the original beauty. Therefore in 1975 a new version was commissioned. Many experts worked on it and finally it was published in 1982.

Read this text carefully in order to fix in your mind what is described.

> [1] Immediately, in the morning, the chief priests held a consultation with the elders and scribes and the whole council; and they bound Jesus, led *Him* away, and delivered *Him* to Pilate. [2] Then Pilate asked Him, "Are You the King of the Jews?" He answered and said to him, *"It is as* you say." [3] And the chief priests accused Him of many things, but He answered nothing. [4] Then Pilate asked Him

---

[33] Scripture taken from the *New King James Version*, copyright © 1982 Thomas Nelson, Inc., used with permission; all rights reserved.

again, saying, "Do You answer nothing? See how many things they testify against You!" ⁵ But Jesus still answered nothing, so that Pilate marvelled. ⁶ Now at the feast he was accustomed to releasing one prisoner to them, whomever they requested. ⁷ And there was one named Barabbas, *who was* chained with his fellow rebels; they had committed murder in the rebellion. ⁸ Then the multitude, crying aloud, began to ask *him to do* just as he had always done for them. ⁹ But Pilate answered them, saying, "Do you want me to release to you the King of the Jews?" ¹⁰ For he knew that the chief priests had handed Him over because of envy. ¹¹ But the chief priests stirred up the crowd, so that he should rather release Barabbas to them. ¹² Pilate answered and said to them again, "What then do you want me to do *with Him* whom you call the King of the Jews?" ¹³ So they cried out again, "Crucify Him!" ¹⁴ Then Pilate said to them, "Why, what evil has He done?" But they cried out all the more, "Crucify Him!" ¹⁵ So Pilate, wanting to gratify the crowd, released Barabbas to them; and he delivered Jesus, after he had scourged *Him*, to be crucified.

Reading

Among the Gospel writers only Matthew interrupts the transfer of Jesus to Pilate with the haunting tale of the remorse and suicide of Judas. After the betrayal in the garden of Gethsemane, Mark mentions this tragic figure no more. It is not completely clear where Pilate questioned Jesus. It seems most likely that it was the Herodian Palace that stood on top of the western hill of Jerusalem, and not the Fortress Antonia of the medieval and modern "Way of the Cross".[34] Pontius Pilate was the Roman Prefect or Governor, representative of the Emperor, from 26-36 A.D. which covers the time of Jesus' public ministry and death. Unsurprisingly Pilate was not a popular figure among the people of Judea as he represented the occupying power, and it seems that he had been unnecessarily cruel from time to time. He certainly would not have baulked at savagely putting down any hint of a rebellion against Rome.

This scene is another instance of the prophecy of Jesus coming true. He had said that the Son of Man would be handed over to the pagans (10:33). From the story that the Gospel writers present it seems that Pilate could see clearly that Jesus was innocent of any crime in the sense of Roman law. He would not have

---
34 Brown, *op. cit.*, Vol. I, p. 635.

been at all interested in what were to him arcane religious matters, but he was swayed by political pressure.

The Gospels do not provide a legal report of the trial nor an eyewitness summary. There is an historical core in what the Gospels say, but they are more concerned to present the meaning of the events for believers. The Gospels are not concerned with our modern day questions and therefore do not tell us everything we might like to know. Pilate sentenced Jesus to die on the cross on the charge of being "the King of the Jews". The title is Pilate's way of understanding the Jewish idea of messiah. The Gospels are not interested in who told Pilate what, but in proclaiming who Jesus really is. The question of Pilate – "Are you the King of the Jews?" – is identical in all four Gospels, and Jesus' answer – "It is as you say" – is the same in the Synoptic Gospels (*Mark* 15:2; *Matthew* 27:11; *Luke* 23:3) while in John's Gospel, Jesus answers with another question (*John* 18:33-34). The answer of Jesus is not quite as direct as it might seem in the translation we are using for this Station, and indeed is not direct in any of the Gospels. This hints that Christians see both true and false aspects of Jesus as King of the Jews.[35] Jesus is indeed a king but not like earthly kings. His kingdom is of a completely different order, and he has no interest in establishing political domination.

Another common element is that when Pilate continues questioning Jesus, he does not respond. This would have reminded those who knew the Scriptures of the prophecy regarding the Suffering Servant in *Isaiah*: "Harshly dealt with, he bore it humbly, he never opened his mouth, like a lamb that is led to the slaughter-house, like a sheep that is dumb before its shearers never opening its mouth" (53:7).

The scene Mark paints would also remind the first readers of the just one in the psalm who is surrounded by enemies who speak words of hate (*Psalm* 109:2-3). The chief priests accuse Jesus of many other things in front of Pilate who seems to ignore them, and who addresses himself once again to Jesus (*Mark* 15:4-5). However, Jesus does not answer a word, to Pilate's amazement.

In the Roman trial we have the initial questioning by Pilate that we can find in all four Gospels: *Mark* 15:2-5; *Matthew* 27:11-14; *Luke* 23:2-5; *John* 18:28b-38a. The Roman trial of Jesus is treated differently in each Gospel, but there are elements of the Christian tradition that are common to all. In St. Mark's Gospel the whole Roman trial runs from *Mark* 15:1-15 and is just over half the length of the proceedings before the Sanhedrin. Pilate is portrayed as a weak man, but

---

35 cf. *Ibid.*, Vol. I, pp. 729-30.

not as guilty as the chief priests and the Sanhedrin. Matthew greatly expands the scenes before Pilate (27:1-26) while using Mark's story as a basis. Luke's account (23:1-25) is about the same length as Matthew and he too uses Mark's material but has reshaped it drastically. John presented the shortest account of Jesus before the Jewish authorities (18:13-27), while his Roman trial is three times the length of that in Mark (18:28–19:16a).[36]

Mark does not mention the episode that Luke records of Jesus being sent to Herod and being interrogated by him (*Luke* 23:6-12). Brown suggests that this story reflects a Christian tradition that Herod's opposition to Jesus played some part in the death of Jesus.[37]

All the four Gospels agree that the Romans had in custody a prisoner named Barabbas (*Mark* 15:7; *Matthew* 27:16; *Luke* 23:19; *John* 18:40b). It is not entirely clear why he was held. Mark has the basic story about the crowd asking Pilate to release one prisoner as apparently was the custom at the time of the Passover feast. According to Mark and Matthew, this seems to have been a Roman custom, which is unlikely. In John's Gospel there is perhaps a more plausible explanation, that the Jewish people would ask for the release of prisoners at Passover. Pilate offered to release "the King of the Jews", i.e. Jesus, but the chief priests stirred up the crowd to ask for the release of Barabbas instead. Matthew mostly follows Mark's story. Luke has several different elements. Mark wants to point out the contrast between the release of a guilty rioter and the crucifixion of one completely innocent of any such political involvement.[38] No Gospel explains why the people wanted to have Barabbas released rather than Jesus. The name "Barabbas" means "son of the father", so the choice is ironic between Jesus, who is the only Son of the Father, or this Barabbas. There is no mention of even one voice raised in favour of Jesus. In all the Gospels the mass opposition to him is what ultimately forces Pilate to accede to the crucifixion.[39]

The opposition of the crowd is strange, given that a short time previously the people had welcomed Jesus into Jerusalem with cries of "Hosanna" (11:9-10), although it was the people who entered the city with him who greeted him in this way, not the inhabitants. Pope Benedict clearly says: "The crowd that paid homage to Jesus at the gateway to the city was not the same crowd that later demanded his crucifixion."[40] Jesus had never courted popularity, and while he had aroused the great opposition of the leaders, it seems from the rest of the

---
36 *Ibid.*, Vol. I, pp. 753-59.
37 *Ibid.*, Vol. I, pp. 778-86.
38 *Ibid.*, Vol. I, p. 797.
39 *Ibid.*, Vol. I, p. 809.
40 Pope Benedict XVI, *Jesus of Nazareth, op. cit.*, p. 8.

Gospel that he was very popular among the ordinary people, although they may have expected him to be different from his own understanding of his mission (cf. 8:27-30). When the people saw him bound, beaten and in the power of the Romans, they may have thought that Barabbas would make a better messiah than Jesus. Their hopes in Jesus were disappointed and they reacted with fury.

In the Gospels it seems that Pilate does not want to have Jesus crucified but feels constrained to do so by the pressure of the crowd. Matthew has the famous scene of Pilate washing his hands as a sign that he is innocent of the blood of Jesus. Pilate hands Jesus over to be flogged in Mark and Matthew and then crucified. In Luke's version, he states that he will release Jesus after having him whipped. John's story is much longer and more dramatic. The usual Roman practice when flogging a criminal was to strip him and bind him to a low post or throw him to the ground. The implement was usually of leather ending in five points each of which had a piece of metal or stone, and the beating was expected to be savage. This punishment was also used to inflict the death penalty. Being spat upon, mocked and scourged fulfils Jesus' own prediction (10:33-34).

Although Jesus is sentenced to death by the representative of Rome and it is carried out according to their barbaric customs, perhaps the early Christians had a hand in apportioning blame for the death of Jesus. The Gospels play up the role of the chief priests and the crowd demanding that Jesus be crucified. It is never stated that he is condemned for treason or sedition, and so it might have been believed that this would encourage the Roman Empire not to persecute the followers of Jesus. If this were the reason for downplaying the role of the Romans in the death of Jesus, it was not very successful as later persecutions showed.

Reflecting

Pilate can seemingly see clearly that Jesus is innocent, but because of political pressure Pilate feels that his hands are tied. He tries to acquit Jesus but fails. Political expediency comes before a human life. Pilate is a tragic figure of history. He allowed Jesus to be crucified because he refused a take a stand against injustice. We may not actively do much evil in our lives, but how much evil do we allow to happen because we are not prepared to stand up and prevent it?

Jesus was crucified by the Roman authorities and a man of violence was released. Some people have proposed that Jesus was a Zealot, a man who tried to lead a violent revolution against the Roman occupiers. That is certainly not the impression that the Gospels give. Indeed Pope Benedict states that, "Violence does not build up the kingdom of God, the kingdom of humanity. On the contrary, it is a favourite instrument of the Antichrist, however idealistic its religious motivation may be. It serves not humanity but inhumanity."[41]

The people are given the choice between Barabbas and Jesus. This is a choice that appears before every generation and before every human being: will you accept the way God works, in humility and self-giving love, or do you want to construct a human kingdom with human methods?

I will propose some more questions that might help you take this piece of Scripture into your heart so that it might bear fruit in your life.

1. What do you do when you feel that you are being pressurised to make a decision that you feel is not right?
2. Who are the people and what are the things that might bring pressure to bear on you?
3. Why do you think that God allowed Jesus to be condemned to death?

Pilate's story

I will not be questioned by anyone! I am in charge here. I wish that I were in Rome instead of this backwater, but I am a soldier and I will do my duty. I don't want to risk stories getting back to Caesar that I cannot control this place. All he wants are the taxes to flow into his coffers and that the 'Pax Romana', the peace that the Empire brings, shows these barbarians the benefits of being under Rome's gentle heel.

I am not to blame. His own people brought him to me. They wanted him dead. What a bloodthirsty lot. Crucifixion is not nice, I can assure you, but nothing less would satisfy them. He was a strange one. He barely spoke. He never defended himself. Seemed to think that he was a king. At first I thought he was mad but he wasn't. He seemed to be very calm even though he stood before my tribunal and his own people were baying for his blood.

What was I supposed to do? They were going to inform Caesar that I was not up to the job. I couldn't have that. I don't want to be here but I don't want to go back in disgrace. It was only one man. Who cares?

---

41 *Ibid.*, p. 15.

Responding

Read the text of Scripture again that we have been focusing on. Read it slowly. There is a lot in it. We have tried to take it in and reflect on it. Now is the time to have a heart-to-heart conversation with God. This piece of Scripture may have set-off all sorts of thoughts in you. Speak to God from your heart now.

To start the dialogue, perhaps the following prayer (*Psalm* 139) may get you going. If you want to get right in to opening your heart to God that is great; skip the prayer.

> [1] O LORD, You have searched me and known *me*.
>
> [2] You know my sitting down and my rising up; You understand my thought afar off.
>
> [3] You comprehend my path and my lying down, and are acquainted with all my ways.
>
> [4] For *there is* not a word on my tongue, *but* behold, O LORD, You know it altogether.
>
> [5] You have hedged me behind and before, and laid Your hand upon me.
>
> [6] *Such* knowledge *is* too wonderful for me; It is high, I cannot *attain* it.
>
> [7] Where can I go from Your Spirit? Or where can I flee from Your presence?
>
> [8] If I ascend into heaven, You *are* there; If I make my bed in hell, behold, You *are there*.
>
> [9] *If* I take the wings of the morning, *and* dwell in the uttermost parts of the sea,
>
> [10] Even there Your hand shall lead me, and Your right hand shall hold me.
>
> [11] If I say, "Surely the darkness shall fall on me," Even the night shall be light about me;
>
> [12] Indeed, the darkness shall not hide from You, but the night shines as the day; The darkness and the light *are* both alike *to You*.
>
> [13] For You formed my inward parts; You covered me in my mother's womb.

Resting

When you have shared with God what is in your heart, the long Christian tradition suggests that you take some time to rest in the Word of God. This resting goes beyond your words, your thoughts and your feelings. We do have difficulty staying in this silent place because our minds are so active. We feel that we must be doing something. Various methods of prayer have been proposed, particularly in the last few years, to help us stay in the silence. Some have been influenced by non-Christian religions, and others have their roots in the very rich Christian contemplative tradition that many people were completely unaware of. It is useful to be aware of where your own particular method of prayer comes from. Christian prayer is a relationship with God in Christ through the Holy Spirit. You can address any Person of the Trinity, and in this way you are entering into relationship with God. Christ came that we might have life, and it would be foolish to ignore this offer.

Many methods of prayer help us to listen. We must do something about our own false self that tends to distort what we hear and is in competition with everyone else for a slice of the cake. The method of prayer that I want to propose here is often called 'Centering Prayer'.[42] I propose it not because it is better than all the other methods, or more efficacious, but because I have found it helpful over many years.

There are some basic guidelines to help one get into this way of prayer. They are not hard and fast rules, and they certainly do not work by magic. Following the guidelines helps us to make the silence fruitful. The guidelines are:

1. **Choose a Sacred Word as the symbol of your intention to consent to the presence and action of God within.**

   The 'sacred word' is a word that is sacred to you; something that is very meaningful to you in your own relationship with God. People often choose traditionally "holy" words like "Lord", "God", "Father", "Jesus", "Spirit", "Kyrie", "Abba", etc. However, perhaps a word like "Yes" or "Peace" might be highly significant for you. Spend a moment now and ask the Holy Spirit to inspire you to choose a word that is sacred for you.

---

[42] See Thomas Keating, *Open Mind, Open Heart: The Contemplative Dimension of the Gospel*, (Rockport, Massachusetts: Element Books, 1991). See also the other books by Thomas Keating in the official website of *Contemplative Outreach Inc.*, which he founded – www. contemplativeoutreach.org – as well as the official website in the United Kingdom: www.couk.org.uk. For a simple introduction to Centering Prayer, see Elizabeth Smith and Joseph Chalmers, *A Deeper Love: An Introduction to Centering Prayer*, (London & New York: Continuum, 1999).

During Centering Prayer, this word will be the symbol of your intention to consent to the presence and action of God in your life. This method of prayer is one of *intention* and not *attention*. Therefore it is a prayer of the heart and not so much of the mind. Sometimes our minds can be still when we are at prayer, but very often they are filled with distractions. When our prayer has been distracted we can feel bad, but in Centering Prayer it is the *intention* that matters. Therefore what do you really want? What do you desire? If you desire to think about what your next meal is going to be then that is your intention. However, if you really desire God, no matter how often you have been distracted, your intention does not change.

2. **Sitting comfortably and with eyes closed, settle briefly, and silently introduce the 'sacred word' as the symbol of your intention to consent to God's presence and action.**

Sit comfortably in a way that you do not have to move around every few seconds, but sit in a way that you remain alert. If you lie on your bed, do not be surprised if you go to sleep!

At the beginning of the time you have decided to dedicate to the period of Centering Prayer, very gently introduce the sacred word that you have chosen under the influence of the Holy Spirit. Do not say it out loud or even mentally. Just let it arise from within you. God hears what is in your heart. It is the symbol of your consent to what God is doing within you.

3. **When you become aware that you are engaged with your thoughts, return ever so gently to the Sacred Word.**

The 'sacred word' is not a mantra and is not repeated all the time; we only return to it when we become aware that we are caught up with one thought or another. People who are alive have thoughts, so do not be concerned if you have thoughts during the time of prayer! Perhaps over time you will be able to let your thoughts come and let them go without getting caught up with them. When you become aware that you are thinking about whatever, then you make a split second decision either to continue thinking about that most interesting topic or returning your heart to God. If you decide to continue thinking about the football match or what you are going to eat, then your decision has changed and it is no longer prayer. If, however, you decide that you do want to stay in God's presence, all you have to do is allow the sacred word that you have chosen as the symbol of your consent to God's presence and action in your life to arise in your heart. God knows what you mean.

4. **At the end of the prayer period, remain in silence for a few minutes with eyes closed.**

This is a very practical guideline to help you bring the fruit of your prayer into daily life. It is not a good idea to jump up immediately and throw yourself into some frenetic activity. Take your time.

What's Next?

We started off this Station with Pilate and him caving into pressure. As a result, Jesus was condemned to death. Our decisions do matter. Today try to be aware of your judgements of other people and how your decisions might affect them.

*Jesus is crowned with thorns.
Ceramic by Adam Kossowski on the Rosary Way at Aylesford Priory, Kent,
marking the Third Sorrowful Mystery.*

The Eighth Station

JESUS IS CROWNED WITH THORNS

Mark 15:16-20a

Prayer

Jesus, you brought the love of God to our world and yet we responded with blows and derision. The world does not accept your message. Let us live according to your way of self-sacrificing love in the confident faith that only this way leads to life. Amen.

Text

The translation of this part of the story of the Passion comes from the *Good News Bible* (*GNB*).[43] The original idea behind this version of the Bible was that it be easily understandable by all, non-native English speakers and children alike. It began life in the U.S.A. as the *Good News Translation*. It is a very popular version of the Bible.

Read the short text slowly in order to have in your mind the details of what happened to Jesus.

> [16] The soldiers took Jesus inside to the courtyard of the governor's palace and called together the rest of the company. [17] They put a purple robe on Jesus, made a crown out of thorny branches, and put it on his head. [18] Then they began to salute him: "Long live the King of the Jews!" [19] They beat him over the head with a stick, spat on him, fell on their knees, and bowed down to him. [20] When they had finished mocking him, they took off the purple robe and put his own clothes back on him.

Reading

The action now moves inside the praetorium, here translated as the governor's palace. This is the first time that this place has been mentioned in the Synoptic Gospels, while for John the whole trial before Pilate takes place inside or outside

---

[43] *Good News Bible*, British Usage Edition, copyright © British & Foreign Bible Society, 1976, 1994. Scriptures quoted are from the *Good News Bible* © 1994 published by the Bible Societies/HarperCollins Publishers Ltd. U.K., *Good News Bible* © American Bible Society 1966, 1971, 1976, 1992. Used with permission.

JESUS IS CROWNED WITH THORNS

the palace. Luke does not report on the precise elements of how the Roman soldiers mocked Jesus except when he was already on the cross. He adds the element of Jesus being mocked by Herod's soldiers. Matthew's story is very similar to that of Mark but adds that a reed is placed in the hand of Jesus. The crown of thorns that the soldiers put on Jesus' head was evidently intended as part of the mockery of the claims that Jesus was king of the Jews. This mockery soon turns to physical abuse. Both Mark and Matthew tell us that Jesus had been dressed in some sort of purple robe which presumably was intended to deride the royal pretensions of Jesus.

This would have once again reminded those who read or listened to the Gospel story of the Suffering Servant: "Without beauty, without majesty we saw him, no looks to attract our eyes; a thing despised and rejected by men, a man of sorrows and familiar with suffering, a man to make people screen their faces; he was despised and we took no account of him." (*Isaiah* 53:2-3); also, "For my part, I made no resistance, neither did I turn away. I offered my back to those who struck me, my cheeks to those who tore at my beard; I did not cover my face against insult and spittle." (*Isaiah* 50:5-6). It also fulfilled another part of Jesus' own prophecy of what would happen to him (10:34), that he would be handed over to the pagans who would mock at him, spit at him, scourge him and put him to death.

When the soldiers were done with their mockery, they had his own clothes put on him. Normally a criminal who had been sentenced to crucifixion would go naked to the place of execution, carrying the lateral beam of his cross. Raymond Brown suggests that Jesus might indeed have been clothed as a concession to the Jewish abhorrence of public nudity.[44]

According to Mark's version of the story, the whole cohort was brought together, although that is not very clear from the translation we are using for this Station. The cohort could have numbered up to six hundred men but such a gathering seems unlikely. Perhaps it means that a large group of soldiers gathered round to watch the spectacle. Purple was the royal colour but it is unlikely that the soldiers would have had access to such a robe. Matthew says it was a scarlet cloak (*Matthew* 27:28). This could have been what the ordinary soldiers wore and is more likely.

---

44 Brown, *op. cit.*, Vol. I, p. 870.

Reflecting

The soldiers mock Jesus, dressing him as a king. They do not recognise who he is, because they have eyes but they cannot see, and ears but they cannot hear. Without faith, all they see is a poor madman who thinks he is a king and who has been condemned to death for his trouble. He is at their mercy, and they show no mercy. They treat him as a thing given for their amusement.

We have been blessed with the eyes of faith. We can see beyond the external appearances to the heart of the matter. In the famous Last Judgement scene towards the end of Matthew's Gospel, the criterion for judgement is how one has treated one's neighbour, and particularly the least (*Matthew* 25:31-46). We can have no excuses because we know that each person has been lovingly created by God and that Christ's blood has been shed for him or her. Whatever we do, even to the most obscure, powerless, weakest member of the human race, we do to Christ. He stands solidly with the poor and oppressed people of this world. God has thrown down the proud from their thrones and exalted the lowly. As followers of Christ, we are called to spread the Good News above all to the poor, the news that each human life is precious in the eyes of the Lord and that each person is loved by God. They will believe this only if they are shown concrete proof. Who is going to show them?

Why did Mark relate this story about the brutal treatment meted out to the Lord? Jesus was laughed at and treated in a disgusting and cruel fashion because he had been condemned for claiming to be a king. The first Christians knew that Jesus in fact is the King and Lord of the whole of creation. However, Jesus came into possession of his kingdom with blows and wearing a crown of thorns. This would be a sure antidote for all Christians against any pretension and tendency to lord it over others, or seeking earthly and political power.

Throughout the history of Christianity there have been dark and bright moments. There have been some wonderful examples and people who really take seriously Christ's message and his pattern of humility; but also, with sorrow, we have to recognise that there have been others who do not. Jesus challenged his contemporaries and all those who would come after to take up their cross and follow him. The cross does not mean only the difficulties, big or small, we have to face in our lives. The cross was the destiny that Jesus embraced. He came into the world to make the self-sacrificing love of God present to all people. It is to this same self-sacrificing love that he invites all those who wish to follow him. There are very many different ways of living-out in practice this kind of love, but they will all have a taste of the cross at some

JESUS IS CROWNED WITH THORNS

point because it goes against the grain. Selfishness is part and parcel of every human being, and this part of us – often called the false self – does not want to sacrifice itself, so it struggles against every attempt to love as God loves.

The following questions are intended to help you grow in your life of following Jesus. Take your time with them. There are no right or wrong answers, just your answers before God.

1. Can you think of a time when you were cruel to someone else in word or deed? Ask God to bless that person now.
2. What do you think causes people to be cruel to each other?
3. Why do you think the soldiers were so cruel to Jesus, and why did God the Father not stop it?

Story of one of the soldiers

Don't look at me like that. I hate it here. We all do. It's the worst detail I've had as a soldier and there is nothing to do. We just crucify a few criminals sometimes. We keep the peace, but I became a soldier to fight. They all hate us, but they're too scared to fight.

This guy thought he was a king. His own people wanted him dead. All their priests brought him to Pilate to be condemned to death. They really hated him. Crucifixion is not nice. Somebody told me that Pilate didn't really want to condemn the poor man, but in the end he agreed with the demands of the Jewish leaders. Who knows why? Who cares?

Somebody who is going to be crucified is flogged. I've been flogged a few times but nothing like this. The guy was beaten to a pulp. He could hardly stand. We don't have much fun so we all gathered round to watch. One of my mates had a great idea to put a cloak round him because he was a king. Then another one of the soldiers made a crown for him from the thorn plant and stuck it on his head. Then we took it in turns to kneel before him. It may have got a bit out of hand but once we had the guy at our mercy some of the men went crazy. We didn't want him to die on us before the sentence could be carried out. That was the only reason we stopped.

Responding

We have tried to ponder on this scene of the soldiers mocking Jesus, and to find how it might apply to our own lives. Now is the moment to leave aside our thoughts and this book. Now is the moment to let our heart speak directly to the heart of God. We do not need formal prayers at this point or big words. Just let what you really feel flow out.

The following psalm (109) might help to start you off:

> [1] God whom I praise, do not be silent!
>
> [2] Wicked and deceiving words are being said about me, false accusations are cast in my teeth.
>
> [3] Words of hate fly all around me, though I give no cause for hostility.
>
> [4] In return for my friendship they denounce me, and all I can do is pray!
>
> [5] They repay my kindness with evil, and friendship with hatred.

Resting

There is a time to ponder on the Word of God, to read it, think about it, meditate upon it and pray about it. There is also a time to rest in the Word, letting go of our own ideas and concerns. There can be the sense of doing nothing, and the temptation to once again do something and then be in control of what we do when we pray. However, prayer is a relationship, and in a good relationship there is time for speaking and time for listening. Resting in the Word of God is a way to listen at a profound level.

In the previous Station I presented a method of prayer that is often called 'Centering Prayer'. It could also be called the prayer of consent or of desire. It is certainly not the only way to listen to God at a deep level; there are several other methods of prayer to help us stay attentive in silence. Each person can find his or her own way to best listen. If you think that you need do nothing to improve your listening skills as they are perfectly adequate already, perhaps you need to think again. All of us have a lot of internal noise that makes it difficult to really hear what another person is saying to us.

By internal noise I mean the commentaries that go on within us non-stop about everything we see or whatever pops into our head. When it comes to listening to God, it is even more difficult because God does not speak as human beings do. The Word of God is "something alive and active. It cuts more finely than any double-edged sword." (*Hebrews* 4:12). This means that the Word of God touches a very profound place within us if we allow it. At the beginning of the spiritual journey, God cannot touch us deeply as we have no depths to touch. God has to excavate these depths first of all, and this is not always pleasant. In the silence God may point out to us something that we have been unable or unwilling to face. In daily life we can escape the voice of God by filling our lives with things and with noise. A constant barrage of noise effectively puts up a barrier to God who will not force us to listen but always invites us to be aware that there is something more than what is obvious. The Carmelite St. Teresa of Avila wrote that prayer and meditation were the way to enter within oneself.[45] God can intrude in one's life at any time in any place, but presumably most people just shrug off the strange experience, whatever it may be. Usually they cannot forget about it completely, but they never seek to understand its cause or meaning. If, however, one does respond to the experience by seeking to enter within through prayer and meditation, then we open the way to a dialogue with God at a profound level. In this way we are expressing our great interest in our relationship with God.

Take a moment now for silence. Read the Scripture text we have been meditating on and then have some time in silence, not to think about what happened to Jesus but simply to spend time in his presence. Our silence can be very eloquent.

What's Next?

What do we do when we have come to the end of the period that we have decided to dedicate to prayer? The relationship with God cannot be limited to a relatively short period of time in the day. If it is authentic our prayer will have an effect on our life. How about today refusing to put anyone down, no matter what we may think of that person? The soldiers presumably thought that Jesus was a madman and a criminal and they mocked him as king. As regards the last, little did they know how close they were to the truth.

---

[45] St. Teresa of Avila, *Interior Castle*, *op.cit.*, 1.5-7.

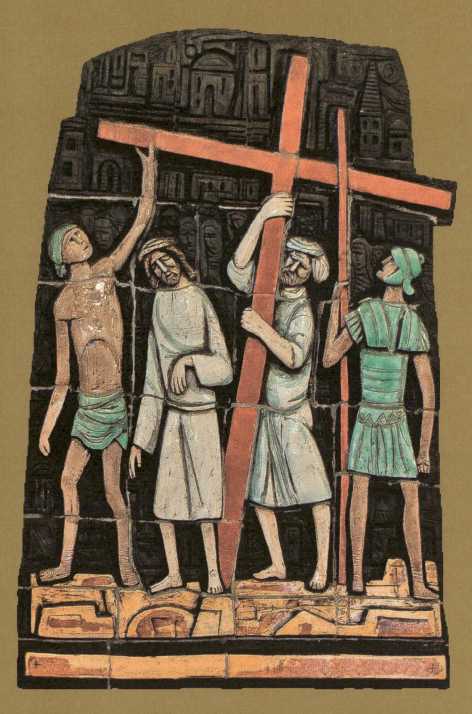

Simon of Cyrene helps Jesus carry the cross.
Fifth Station in the Relic Chapel at Aylesford Priory.
Ceramic by Adam Kossowski.

The Ninth Station

THE WAY OF THE CROSS

Mark 15:20b-21

Prayer

Oh God, your Son was condemned to death for our sake and Simon was pressed into service to help him carry his cross to the place of execution. Help me to be aware when I am asked to share Christ's burden to take it up gladly so that your will may be done. Amen.

Text

The text below is taken from a commentary on Mark's Gospel.[46] The authors have tried to be straightforward and simple. Their goal was to capture the vividness and flow of Mark's story without translating everything literally.

Read this short text now to fix in your mind what is happening and who are the characters involved.

> [20b] and they led him away to crucify him.
>
> [21] And they pressed into service a passer-by, a certain Simon of Cyrene, coming in from the countryside, the father of Alexander and Rufus, to carry his cross.

Reading

Common to all the Gospels is a description of Jesus being led outside the city to be crucified and the carrying of the cross, either by Simon or by Jesus himself. Luke adds that Jesus is followed by a crowd of people including some women to whom Jesus addresses a prophecy of woe (*Luke* 23:27-31). Shortly after Jesus died, Herod Agrippa built another wall around Jerusalem, which considerably enlarged the city to the north so that the place where Jesus died was then incorporated into the city.[47]

---

[46] John R. Donahue, S.J., & Daniel J. Harrington, S.J., 'The Gospel of Mark', *Sacra Pagina*, Volume 22, (A Michael Glazier Book published by Liturgical Press, Collegeville, Minnesota, 2002).

[47] Brown, *op. cit.*, Vol. II, p. 913.

Normally the vertical part of the cross was already standing at the place of execution and the criminal would himself carry the crossbeam. Brown tells that us that often this beam was carried behind the nape of the neck like a yoke, with the condemned man's arms pulled back and hooked over it. The first Christians, unlike later artists, would have understood that Jesus was forced to carry the crossbeam and not the whole cross.[48] It was this that was given to Simon to carry for Jesus.

The Synoptic Gospels all mention that Simon of Cyrene (in the area of present-day Libya) carried the cross for Jesus. From his name he was very likely Jewish, but one who normally lived outside of Israel or who had come from outside to live in the homeland. Not only does Mark mention his name, but also the names of his sons, Alexander and Rufus, presumably because they were well-known within Mark's Christian community. Saint Paul mentions someone called Rufus who was a member of the Christian community in Rome (*Romans* 16:13). It was a fairly common name in Latin, but there is the tradition that Mark wrote his Gospel for the Church in Rome so there might be a connection there.

We are told that Simon was "coming in from the countryside". The original Greek could also mean "coming in from the fields". This seems to suggest either that Simon was just finishing his work, or that he had made a journey, both of which would have been against the Jewish law on the Passover. This might support the dating of the crucifixion that we find in John's Gospel to the eve of the Passover rather than the feast itself (see the second and third Stations for a discussion of a dating of when Jesus died). It seems that Simon did not know Jesus at this point and that he was coerced into carrying the cross for Jesus. This would have been unusual because part of the condemned man's punishment was to carry his own cross to the place of execution. Doubtless we can exclude the possibility that the Roman soldiers took pity on Jesus. However, it may have occurred if Jesus were becoming dangerously weak and the soldiers might have feared that he would die before the execution could be carried out. John's Gospel does not mention Simon at all and states that Jesus carried his own cross (*John* 19:17).

All the parts of the Passion story are included not just to satisfy curiosity but for a theological purpose, that is, through these stories we learn a little bit more about who Jesus is and what is the purpose of his suffering and death. The crucifixion itself is mentioned very sparingly, while other details are described more fully, but these are all interpreted in the light of what the Psalms in

---

48 *Ibid.*

particular tell of the innocent man who is persecuted (*Psalm* 22). Only in this way could the first Christian community make sense of what had happened to Jesus. Therefore the story of the Passion is not an account of an execution, nor a pious and moving religious tale, but is the proclamation of the saving death of Jesus. The death of this just one gives hope to all, especially those who are persecuted down through the ages.

The first readers or hearers of the Gospel would have taken courage from this little story of Simon because they too were persecuted and had to carry their cross. In doing so they were carrying the cross of the Saviour.

Reflecting

Saint Paul wrote to the Galatians, "Bear one another's burdens and then you will be fulfilling the law of Christ" (*Galatians* 6:2). Simon of Cyrene was forced to bear the burden of Christ on his way to the cross. If we wish to be followers of Christ we must accept our cross whatever that may be. This is not a depressing asceticism, but the only way to live a fully human life is to face up to the challenge of being human. By means of adversity we become like gold in the crucible. All that makes us less than human is burned away until what is left is pure gold. Then we are fitted to take our place in the new creation. Saint Paul also wrote, "If in union with Christ we have imitated his death, we shall also imitate him in his resurrection." (*Romans* 6:5).

The cross in the Christian life is inescapable. Jesus willingly accepted it but does ask his followers to share the burden. He came to reveal the love of God to humanity and this is a kind of love that seeks nothing for itself but is essentially self-sacrificing. God does not love you and me because of any merit that we have been able to pile up in the heavenly bank or because of any natural quality that we possess. God loves us because God loves us. That was not a typographical error but really is the nature of God's way of loving – to love with no motive. We who are called to follow Jesus have the vocation to become transformed so that we will love as God loves, for no reason and with no motive.

Will we ever arrive at that? Only God knows, but the important thing is that we are on the way. We are in a process of being transformed. In order to proceed on this way we have to accept that this way of loving can have consequences. Jesus shared the love of God with the poor, with sinners, with the outcasts, and this troubled those who held power and who seemed to believe that they were the controllers of the divine love. Because Jesus was out of control they crucified

THE WAY OF THE CROSS

him. Usually we very strictly control who will receive our love. Once it goes out of control, who knows what will happen?

The following questions might help you to apply the little text of Scripture we have been thinking about to your own life.

1. Whom do you love? Stop for a moment and pray for the ones you love.
2. Who is definitely outside the scope of your love?
3. How would Jesus react to these people?
4. Is he asking you to change in any way?

Simon's story

I was angry and a bit frightened too. The Romans can make us do whatever they want. That's the price we pay for being an occupied nation. I used to pray for liberation and that God's Kingdom would be established with the defeat of all our enemies, but I might have to think again.

I was just coming into the city when I was caught up in a rabble, people who were shouting and swearing and weeping and screaming. You had to be there to appreciate it. Then I found myself at the front and I saw this poor man on the ground. He was going to be executed and was carrying his cross. But he was very weak. One of the soldiers grabbed hold of me and told me to carry the cross for the man. Why me? Surely the man had some friends? But you can't argue with the Roman soldiers so I picked it up. It wasn't light, I can tell you.

I followed behind the man on the way to Golgotha, the usual place of execution. I carried that cross with bad grace at first but something happened on the way. I don't know what it was but I wanted to carry his cross; I wanted to share his burden.

I don't know what to make of the latest news. I stayed and I saw him die. He was dead. He was certainly different from other men. I was angry when they made me carry the cross but I'm glad now.

Responding

The Word of God is addressed to each one of us. We read and listen; we ponder and try to work out its implications for our lives. There comes a time when words become superfluous and the heart takes over. Let your heart speak directly to God now. Take the time you need to share with God what is in your heart.

To get you started you might like to say the following prayer very slowly and then open your heart to God who calls you to an intimate relationship in and through his Son Jesus.

> *Lord, you ask us to carry each other's burdens. Simon was blessed beyond anything he could ever have imagined when he took up the cross of Christ. Hear now the cry of my heart and bless me with your presence ...*

Resting

When we begin our relationship with God, whether we begin as young children or much older, we usually learn vocal prayers. Sometimes people learn prayers as children, but forget them as life takes them far away from God. There is the story of the nurse who gave the fatal injection to Carmelite friar Blessed Titus Brandsma in Dachau concentration camp during World War II. After the war was over, she began to think about what she had done, and she went to the door of a Carmelite house in The Netherlands and told the prior of the community everything she knew about Fr. Titus' last moments. She recounted that Titus gave her his rosary that had been made in the camp, and invited her to use it because she had been brought up as a Catholic. She told him that she could not pray any more. Titus suggested that at least she could say, "Pray for us sinners".[49]

When we begin to take God seriously, prayer takes on a greater importance in our lives. We will tend to use vocal prayers and worshipping with the Christian community will often become a part of our lives. These are the foundations of a good relationship with God. Each of us has a unique relationship with God but we are also part of a people and it is essential for a healthy spiritual life that we remember this. We can support each other with our prayer and service.

As we grow in this relationship with God, prayer will become more and more central in our lives. This does not mean that we will multiply the prayers we say. Vocal prayer will always remain important, but silence will become a normal part of how we relate to God. The silence could be pregnant with meaning, or

---

[49] There is a lot of material about this fascinating Carmelite martyr. See, for example, Joseph Rees, *Titus Brandsma: Modern Martyr*, (London: Sidgwick & Jackson, 1971).

with longing for God who seems to have gone away; it might be expectant as we wait for God to come. We do need a great deal of patience when we pray. Some people want a slot-machine God who will deliver the bar of chocolate on demand, but God is not like that. God is beyond anything we could imagine because God is the source and origin of all that exists and is not part of our world but is the creator of it. True, God sent His Son into the world, but Jesus has ascended now to the right hand of the Father. He left many ways through which we can encounter him: the sacraments, the Word of God, the poor, our neighbour.

God is outside our grasp and God must take the initiative in the relationship. There is nothing we can do to conjure God up like a genie in a bottle. No amount of prayer, no clever technique, or chanting, or whatever we want to do, will make God come to us. We have to wait and not lose patience. Much of prayer, at a certain point, is simply waiting.

There is a beautiful poem that refers to this waiting. It is called *Disclosure*:

> *Prayer is like watching for the Kingfisher.*
> *All you can do is Be where he is likely to appear, and Wait.*
> *Often, nothing much happens;*
> *There is space, silence and Expectancy.*
> *No visible sign, only the Knowledge that he's been there And may come again.*
> *Seeing or not seeing cease to matter,*
> *You have been prepared.*
> *But sometimes, when you've almost Stopped expecting it,*
> *A flash of brightness Gives encouragement.*[50]

Do not lose heart, and be patient. From time to time you may see a flash of brightness. Just be aware that God is present whether you know it or not.

What's Next?

We do not pray to change God's mind or to persuade Him to grant us some little favour. We pray in order to enter into a relationship with God or deepen that relationship. If our prayer really is contact with God, then we will somehow change. We have been meditating on Simon helping Jesus to carry his cross. How about you helping someone to bear the burden that he or she carries? This

---
50 Ann Lewin, *Watching for the Kingfisher: Poems and Prayers*, (Norwich: Canterbury Press, new enlarged edition 2009).

might be an illness or perhaps a lot of work; the burden might be anything. It is important to be delicate when offering your help. Do not assume that the person will welcome your assistance. Ask first and then be willing to do what is necessary.

Jesus is nailed to the cross.
Eleventh Station in the Relic Chapel at Aylesford Priory.
Ceramic by Adam Kossowski.

The Tenth Station

THE CRUCIFIXION

Mark 15:22-27

Prayer

Loving God, Father of Our Lord Jesus Christ, you sent your Son into the world to raise us to the dignity of your sons and daughters. He willingly endured the cross as the price of a love that has no bounds. Help me to experience this love that alone can transform my life. I make this prayer through Christ Our Lord. Amen.

Text

The translation of the next bit of the Passion story is taken from *The Revised English Bible*.[51] This is a revision of the *New English Bible*, which had been published in 1961. The revision was a fully ecumenical venture. The style of English is intended to be fluent and appropriate for liturgical use, while remaining intelligible to people from a wide range of ages and backgrounds. Wherever possible, inclusive language has been used in this translation of the Bible.

Please read this text from the Passion of Jesus with care, taking in all the details.

> [22] They brought Jesus to the place called Golgotha, which means 'Place of a Skull', [23] and they offered him drugged wine, but he did not take it. [24] Then they fastened him to the cross. They shared out his clothes, casting lots to see what each should have. [25] It was nine in the morning when they crucified him; [26] and the inscription giving the charge against him read, 'The King of the Jews.' [27] Two robbers were crucified with him, one on his right and the other on his left.

---

[51] *The Revised English Bible With the Apocrypha*, (Oxford University Press & Cambridge University Press, 1989.

THE CRUCIFIXION

Reading

Raymond Brown detects seven parts to this little description according to Mark: (1) the name of the place; (2) the initial offering of wine; (3) the crucifixion; (4) the division of clothes; (5) the time; (6) the inscription of the charge; (7) the crucifixion of two revolutionaries or bandits along with Jesus.[52] Point 5 is found only in Mark's Gospel, while the other Gospels have most of the items, though sometimes in a different order and with different emphases (*Matthew* 27:33-38; *Luke* 23:33-34; *John* 19:17b-24).

It was the custom to crucify people outside the walls of a city, and it was often near a roadside so that the show should act as a warning to other people. Most people believe that the name of the place where Jesus was crucified was because it looked in some way like a skull. In Jerusalem there is a Church of the Holy Sepulchre dedicated to the place of Jesus' death and burial. After reviewing the other places that have been suggested for the site of the crucifixion, Brown declares that "no candidate more credible than the traditional site is likely to emerge."[53]

In the story of the crucifixion according to both Mark and Matthew, Jesus is offered wine twice. At the beginning of the crucifixion process the Roman soldiers offer him sweet wine but he does not drink it. At the end, just before he dies, someone offers him a course, vinegary wine. This is done when people are mocking him, but it is not clear whether this was intended to mock him further. It is another element which is referred to in the Old Testament: "Give strong drink to one who is perishing, and wine to those in bitter distress; let them drink and forget their poverty, and remember their misery no more." (*Proverbs* 31:6-7).

Mark tells us that the first offering of wine was mixed with myrrh. It was very common in ancient days to make wine heavily scented, and presumably the offering was intended to dull Jesus' pain a little. Mark tells us that the soldiers offered the wine to Jesus. This might be another way to show up the Romans in a better light or perhaps Pilate, who it seems had been impressed by Jesus, might have ordered this little act of mercy. In the garden of Gethsemane, Jesus had prayed that the Father "take this cup" from him, i.e. the cup of suffering, but finally came to accept the Father's will: "let it be as you, not I would have it" (*Mark* 14:36). Therefore, on the cross Jesus wanted to accept the suffering

---

52 cf. Brown, *op.cit.*, Vol. II, p. 935.
53 *Ibid.*, pp. 936-40.

that people threw at him, and at this supreme moment of his life he wanted to be fully aware of what was happening.

The actual crucifixion is described in the briefest possible way: "then they fastened him to the cross" (*Mark* 15:24). Those for whom the Gospel was first written would have been very aware of this most cruel instrument of torture. The Gospel writers were more concerned to show how the suffering and death of Jesus fulfilled the prophecies in the Scripture. None of the Gospels mention the shape of the cross, how Jesus was affixed or any other detail. Crucifixion was a very common form of punishment throughout the ancient world and goes back about seven centuries before Christ. In the Roman Empire, crucifixion was normally reserved to slaves and foreigners. In the *Letter to the Philippians*, we read that Jesus took on the form of a slave and accepted death on a cross (2:7-8). It was considered to be the worst, most degrading and painful form of capital punishment. Scorn was poured on early Christians by pagans for following someone who was executed on a cross.

Criminals were either tied or nailed to the crossbeam, which was then lifted up with the body hanging on it, and placed in the vertical beam. The descriptions of the crucifixion of Jesus in the Gospels do not tell us whether he was tied or nailed, but in *Luke* 24:39 the risen Jesus says, "See my hands and my feet", which would suggest that he had been nailed. *John* 20:25-27 mentions the prints of nails in Jesus' hands. Historical evidence points to the plausibility that Jesus was affixed to the cross with nails through his wrists and his feet. Nails through the fleshy part of his hand would not have held him securely to the cross.

All the Gospels tell us that Jesus' clothes were divided up (*Mark* 15:24b; *Matthew* 27:35b; *Luke* 23:34b; *John* 19:23-24). The normal Roman pattern was to crucify criminals naked, but there may have been an exception in the case of Jews. By custom the soldiers in charge of the crucifixion had the right to divide up the condemned man's clothes. However, the division of the clothes is probably an intended reminder of *Psalm* 22, once again to help the first Christians understand the suffering and death of Jesus as the fulfilment of the Scriptures. In verse 18 we read, "They divided my garments among them and cast lots for my clothes."

Again, despite their different ways of telling the story, the four Gospels agree that the crime with which Jesus was charged was written and seen by those present at the crucifixion (*Mark* 15:26; *Matthew* 27:37; *Luke* 23:38; *John* 19:19-22). He stands accused of presenting himself as "King of the Jews". Again the four Gospels agree that there were two others who were crucified on either side of Jesus (*Mark* 15:27; *Matthew* 27:38; *Luke* 23:33c; *John* 19:18b). Jesus was counted as a common criminal and punished with others. Jesus had protested that when he was arrested in the garden of Gethsemane he was being treated as a bandit, and now he is crucified between two bandits. The word that Mark uses ("robbers") is probably to be understood as revolutionaries, or at least as men who used violence. These robbers were crucified on the right and the left of Jesus, and it seems that we are intended to remember the earlier story when James and John requested to have the places of honour at the right and left of Jesus in his glory. Jesus tells them that these places are not his to grant but belong to those to whom they have been allotted (10:35-40). In the end these places are not allotted to apostles but criminals.

Mark begins to count the hours. He says that it is the third hour, which is translated as nine in the morning. These times responded to the traditional moments of Jewish prayer and they confer on the crucifixion a sacred and liturgical rhythm. Therefore it is not appropriate to try to reconcile the timing of Mark with that in John's Gospel because they are both using time to make different points about the religious significance of the death of Jesus. Neither is simply giving a detailed account of the execution of an innocent man. The different accounts need to be read within their own contexts to really understand the point that each Evangelist wants to make.

You may find verse 28 in your own Bible, which would read something like, "And so the Scripture was accomplished that says: he was counted among the malefactors". This is a reference once again to the figure of the Suffering Servant of *Isaiah* 53:12. This is quoted in Luke's Gospel (22:37). The experts tell us that this verse is very likely a fairly late addition by someone who was copying out the Gospel and who felt it would be good to add this bit. This might act as a warning not to try to add anything to the Gospel as you will be found out!

Reflecting

In John's Gospel, Jesus says: "A man can have no greater love than to lay down his life for his friends" (*John* 15:13). Why did Jesus have to die? He began his public ministry in Galilee, preaching that what was needed to enter the Kingdom of God was a change of heart. He seemed to have great success at first as large crowds followed him everywhere, although the people of his own home village could not accept that the carpenter's son whom they all knew could possibly do the things that were being reported about him (*Mark* 6:1-6). This problem was as nothing compared to the difficulties that were put up by the religious and political leaders from Jerusalem. They thought that he was a blasphemer who posed a real danger to the political stability of the whole country. In the first Station we saw that the chief priests and scribes were looking for a way to arrest Jesus and have him put to death. Clearly Jesus had upset a lot of important people.

From very early on, the followers of Jesus tried to understand what had happened to him through the eyes of Scripture. They found many prophecies which spoke of the mysterious figure of the Servant of God, especially in *Isaiah* (42:1-53:12) and in the Psalms (particularly *Psalm* 22). Through these prophecies the early Christians came to understand that the destiny of Jesus was to die on the cross, and that this was according to the Father's will despite the fact that it was caused by human beings. The whole of the New Testament is a presentation of the Good News about Jesus the Christ who suffered, died and rose again from the dead to break the power of death over human beings. People killed Jesus, thinking they had rid themselves of a problem, but in fact they were helping to bring about precisely what God had decreed: that God would become human so that human beings could participate in the divine life forever. Being human, Jesus had to experience death in order to take away its sting, which was precisely the separation from God. Now death is a gateway to eternal life.

The Gospels and the other parts of the New Testament are faith documents, that is, they are written from the standpoint of faith in the resurrection of Jesus from the dead. They are not just telling stories about a dead hero but they seek to share an understanding of Christ's life in the light of the whole of what we now call the Old Testament. Jesus died because the love of God knows no bounds. He revealed a love that is forgetful of self, that refuses to hate, no matter the provocation. This is the way God loves, and God invites each one of us to participate in this way of loving.

Jesus suffered and died because his love is stronger than hatred, stronger than sin, and ultimately stronger than death.

Human beings make history, but God directs where history is heading. You and I are invited to become tuned-in to God's ways so that we work with God to build the Kingdom. We pray "Thy Kingdom come" and we are invited to co-operate with God in the transformation of the human heart, to make it capable of receiving this Kingdom. We must start with our own heart.

THE CRUCIFIXION

The following questions are intended to help you apply this Station to your own life.

1. What do you think the death of Jesus has accomplished?
2. Why do you think Jesus was rejected?
3. Jesus said that whatever we did even to the least, we did to him. Is there anyone you treat with disdain or cruelty?

The story of an onlooker

That was not the first time I have seen someone crucified. It is always horrible. I don't know what to make of the man. From everything I heard he did some wonderful things. He healed a lot of people and spoke beautifully about God. But these messiahs are dangerous. The Romans need no excuse to crush us. He wasn't a revolutionary, but some of his followers were a bit questionable. There was no sign of them when they stuck him up on the cross. I think he was innocent but I don't know anything about what they are saying about him now.

Responding

I invite you to read again the piece of Scripture we have been meditating on in this Station. Read it slowly, and then pray the following *Psalm* 142 slowly:

¹ With my voice I cry to the LORD; with my voice I make supplication to the LORD.

² I pour out my complaint before him; I tell my trouble before him.

³ When my spirit is faint, you know my way. In the path where I walk they have hidden a trap for me.

⁴ Look on my right hand and see – there is no one who takes notice of me; no refuge remains to me; no one cares for me.

⁵ I cry to you, O LORD; I say, "You are my refuge, my portion in the land of the living."

⁶ Give heed to my cry, for I am brought very low. Save me from my persecutors, for they are too strong for me.

[7] Bring me out of prison, so that I may give thanks to your name. The righteous will surround me, for you will deal bountifully with me.

Now close your eyes and speak to God from your heart. Tell God what you feel. Perhaps this Station has stirred up some memories or an inspiration to pray for someone in particular. Now is the opportunity to share what is in your heart with God.

Resting

What do you expect when you pray? Do you expect God to respond, to answer your prayers in some way? Do you expect God to give you what you have asked for? As a commentary on the *Our Father*, Luke's Gospel tells us of the encouragement that Jesus gave to his followers to be persistent in prayer. First of all Luke describes for us the situation that would have been commonplace to the original hearers. Everyone is in bed in the one room where the whole family slept and a friend comes to the door to borrow something. A guest has arrived unexpectedly and the friend has nothing to give him. The householder does not want to get up and disturb the whole family, but the friend is persistent and gets what he wants. Jesus goes on to say:

> [9] "So I say to you, Ask, and it will be given you; search, and you will find; knock, and the door will be opened for you. [10] For everyone who asks receives, and everyone who searches finds, and for everyone who knocks, the door will be opened. [11] Is there anyone among you who, if your child asks for a fish, will give a snake instead of a fish? [12] Or if the child asks for an egg, will give a scorpion? [13] If you then, who are evil, know how to give good gifts to your children, how much more will the heavenly Father give the Holy Spirit to those who ask him!"
>
> (*Luke* 11:9-13; see also *Matthew* 7:7-11)

Jesus focuses on the faith of the one who prays, not on the particular requests he or she makes. So we have to pray with faith, and we are assured that God will answer our prayers. However, we know by experience that God does not answer all our prayers in the way we expect or hope. Parents usually have a broader vision than their children, and so good parents will not give in to every demand of their children. The reason is because they love them. God loves us more than the best parents love their children, and so God will grant what is really for our good, or for the good of the one for whom we are praying.

It is right to keep asking for whatever it is we seek, but it is also right to accept the answer when that becomes clear to us. In the *Our Father*, we ask that we be given what is necessary for each day, and above all we pray that God's will may be done. When we have had our say and we have pondered on the Scriptures, trying to discern the will of God, there comes a time for silence. This is not an empty silence but one that is full of meaning. We wait in the silence for whatever God may reveal to us. Usually what God wants to say to us is best revealed outside the time of prayer. If we listen at the time of prayer, we will more likely be aware of what God is saying to us in the ordinary events of our daily life.

Take some time to be with God in silence. You have read and pondered the Word of God; you have spoken to God from your heart. Now let God shape and mould you in silence so that your will is attuned to the divine desire.

What's Next?

Jesus started out his mission with such promise. It seems that the local people in general loved him, though his own neighbours could not understand him at all. Now it ends up with Jesus on the cross. Jesus has made it very clear for those who want to follow him that they must take up their cross. Of course, that has been interpreted in many ways, but perhaps one meaning is that we should not be surprised if we come across opposition when we are trying to put God's will into practice. People have done some wonderful things, but also some barbaric things, in the name of God down the centuries. Before you assume that the opposition you face is because you are doing God's will, ask for God's guidance and seek advice from a wise person, which is not necessarily the same as someone who agrees with you.

Jesus dies on the cross.
Twelfth Station in the Relic Chapel at Aylesford Priory.
Ceramic by Adam Kossowski.

The Eleventh Station

JESUS IS MOCKED ON THE CROSS

Mark 15:29-32

Prayer

> *Dear God, your Son revealed your compassionate love for all but it brought him to the cross where he was laughed at as he lay dying. He loved to the end. Help me to appreciate the greatness of this love and to let it transform my way of living. I ask this through Christ Our Lord. Amen.*

Text

Read the following text carefully and make sure you take in all the details. The translation is taken from the *New International Version* (*NIV*).[54] The goals for this translation were that it be accurate, beautiful, clear and dignified, and that it be suitable both for public and private reading.

> [29] Those who passed by hurled insults at him, shaking their heads and saying, "So! You who are going to destroy the temple and build it in three days, [30] come down from the cross and save yourself!" [31] In the same way the chief priests and the teachers of the law mocked him among themselves. "He saved others," they said, "but he can't save himself! [32] Let this Christ, this King of Israel, come down now from the cross, that we may see and believe." Those crucified with him also heaped insults on him.

Reading

The Gospels tell us the reaction of the onlookers at the scene of the crucifixion, and these differ according to the idea that each Evangelist has of the passion. In both Mark and Matthew (*Matthew* 27:39-44) the reactions are completely negative. Three groups are mentioned, and they all mock Jesus. Luke is not completely negative (*Luke* 23:35-43) while John (*John* 19:25-27) has a very positive scene where the small group standing at the foot of the cross, including

---

[54] Scripture taken from the Holy Bible, New International Version, Copyright © 1973, 1978, 1984, International Bible Society. Used by permission of Zondervan. All rights reserved.

JESUS IS MOCKED ON THE CROSS

the mother of Jesus, constitute the believing community from whom Jesus will establish his true family.

Mark presents Jesus as having been misunderstood from the beginning of his public ministry until the very end when he is hanging on the cross. The mocking of the various people is a reminder of *Psalm* 22:8, "All those observing me sneered at me; they spoke with the lips; they wagged the head". They emphasise the powerlessness of Jesus, which has been foreseen, and so enters into God's plan of salvation for the whole world.

Crucifixion was intended to be a public event to humiliate and cruelly kill the condemned man, as well as to drive home the futility of opposing the laws of the Roman Empire. It is not surprising that there were people around the cross of Jesus. The place of crucifixion was probably alongside a road that led in and out of the city gate. Mark's story of the Passion shows Jesus deserted by his friends and ridiculed by everyone else.

The mockery is framed in Scriptural terms. *Psalm* 22 would presumably have been in the mind of Mark as he wrote. This tells of the reaction of the wicked to the just man whom they are persecuting, and his feelings: "But I am a worm, not a man; the scorn of men, despised by the people. All who see me scoff at me; they mock me with parted lips, they wag their heads." (verses 7-8). Also the *Book of Wisdom* (2:16-20) speaks of the persecution of the virtuous man by the ungodly:

> [16] In his opinion we are counterfeit; he avoids our ways as he would filth; he proclaims the final end of the upright as blessed and boasts of having God for his father. [17] Let us see if what he says is true, and test him to see what sort of end he will have. [18] For if the upright man is God's son, God will help him and rescue him from the clutches of his enemies. [19] Let us test him with cruelty and with torture, and thus explore this gentleness of his and put his patience to the test. [20] Let us condemn him to a shameful death since God will rescue him – or so he claims.

In trying to understand what had happened to Jesus and how it fitted in with God's will, his first followers found in passages such as these a great comfort and new light, for despite the disaster it may have appeared, it had been foretold in many places in the Bible.[55]

---

[55] The *Book of Wisdom* was probably written in Greek not in Hebrew, and the Jewish people do not accept it as part of Sacred Scripture. Protestants generally follow this, whereas the Catholic Church accepts it and some other works as part of the Bible. Before they were accepted as being part of the Bible there was a lot of debate, and they are called the 'Deutero-canonical books' to mark them out from the books that

Throughout the Gospel, Jesus has only used his power to accomplish the will of the Father. He had previously warned everyone, "He who wants to save his life will lose it. The one who loses his life for my sake and for the sake of the Gospel will save it." (8:35). The fact that, in Mark's version of the Good News, even those who were crucified with Jesus joined in the abuse, shows his complete isolation on Calvary. Only Luke tells the story of the "good thief" (*Luke* 23:39-43).

Pope Benedict points out the irony of the taunts about Jesus having claimed to destroy the Temple and in three days to build it again, for they do not realise that they are witnessing the destruction of the old Temple and that the new is rising up before them.[56]

The first Christians, and indeed all Christians who have come after them, know that paradoxically, Jesus became the source of salvation for all on the cross. Mark is intent on showing that Jesus is revealed as the Messiah through his suffering and death, and so his version of the Passion has no light until after the death of Jesus. It is important not to try to correct one version of the Gospel with another. Each version of the Passion was written to bring out specific points. There is a remarkable degree of agreement in all four Gospels; they are clearly telling the same story, but they are coming at it from different places and so accentuate one point and perhaps ignore others. We must always remember that these are ancient documents, not written with our ideas in mind or to satisfy our curiosity. These are documents proclaiming Good News from God.

Reflecting

Even on the cross Jesus could not be left alone. The passers-by and the chief priests mocked him. The mystery of God's love for humanity is that Jesus accepted death, even death on a cross. Christ did not cling to his equality with God but emptied himself in order to share our life and our death, so that the chains of death that shackled humanity with fear might be broken.

---

had no question about them ('Proto-canonical'). In Protestant Bibles these books are sometimes left out entirely, or placed at the end under the heading 'Apocrypha'. Therefore Protestants normally have 39 books in the Old Testament, whereas Catholic Bibles have 46. There is no disagreement about what is in the New Testament. If you want to read more about the thorny problem of what should be in or out of the Bible, you can read among others Raymond E. Brown and Raymond F. Collins, 'Canonicity', in *The New Jerome Biblical Commentary*, (eds.) Raymond E. Brown, Joseph A. Fitzmyer & Roland E. Murphy, (London: Geoffrey Chapman, 1989), pp. 1034-54.

56 Pope Benedict XVI, *Jesus of Nazareth*, *op. cit.*, pp. 208-09.

JESUS IS MOCKED ON THE CROSS

The mockers taunted Jesus and expressed their contempt for his powerless state, and at the same time they try to lead him into temptation.[57] Those who ridicule Jesus tempt him to use his divine power to save himself. Jesus expressed his power in powerlessness. It took St. Paul a long time to learn that God's power was actually best expressed in human weakness (cf. *2 Corinthians* 12:7-10).

Pope Benedict mentions an interesting fact that the ancient philosopher Plato (more than 400 years before Christ), in a discussion about justice and injustice, has one of his characters say that if there were a perfectly just person, he would end up by being crucified![58]

Why is it that weakness seems to attract violence? The spread of the Gospel was a huge revolution in the Roman Empire. A central teaching of Jesus was that we love our neighbour and that whatever we do, even for those we consider the least, we do for Christ (*Matthew* 25:31-46). Taking care of the weak was not of central importance to the peoples of ancient times; this was a value introduced by the Judeo-Christian tradition. While it has borne fruit in the development of hospitals, hospices, orphanages and the like, it has not transformed the heart of everyone. Cruelty has always existed, but the Twentieth Century surpassed all that went before in unmitigated evil. Many people seem to reject God in our societies. What will be the effect in the future? What values will shape our culture? A society can be judged by how it treats the weakest members. It seems to be very dangerous for a baby in the womb. Euthanasia, euphemistically called "assisted suicide", is being proposed by some for those who are dying, but where would it stop? A modern commentator worries that some ideas "which at one time would have been rightly regarded by almost anyone as the degenerate ravings of sociopaths, are strangely palatable and even morally compelling to many of their fellows".[59] The founding values of western societies at least are shaped by faith in Jesus and in the message he preached. If people reject Christ and his message, will these values continue to be cherished?

The following questions are intended to help you ponder more deeply the application to your own life of the story about Jesus being mocked while he was on the cross.

1. Saint Paul reported that the Lord told him "My grace is enough for you: my power is at its best in weakness" (*2 Corinthians* 12:9). What does that mean for you?

---

57 *Ibid.*
58 *Ibid.*, p. 210.
59 David Bentley Hart, *Atheist Delusions: The Christian Revolution and its Fashionable Enemies*, (New Haven & London: Yale University Press, 2009).

2. How do you deal with weakness; your own and that of others?
3. Look at a crucifix. Why do you think Jesus attracted so much opposition?

The account of an enemy of Jesus

Hah! Finally we got him! All those stupid people who were following him will listen to us now. They will see that they were led astray by that impostor. The man's disciples were nowhere to be seen; they all ran off when he was arrested. Maybe they will come to their senses now. Some of them were educated and there were rumours that he even had friends among the Sanhedrin. Everyone will see that he was a blasphemer and cursed by God.

Apparently he claimed that he would destroy the Temple and in three days rebuild it. He thought he was a king! How ridiculous! Now he will know that his mission, whatever it was, has failed miserably. He has nothing left. Everything is over. The end of the story!

Responding

The reason for thinking about the Word of God is to let it touch our hearts, that we might grow in our relationship with God. What has the Word said to you? What do you want to say to God? Now is the time to share what is in your heart with God.

To set the conversation rolling, perhaps you could use the opening words of *Psalm 22* which was a very important prayer for the early Christians to understand what had happened to Jesus and why. The psalm speaks of the sufferings of a virtuous man who is persecuted, but it ends with words of hope. Perhaps you would like to pray the whole psalm in your own Bible. Read the psalm, or the opening words of it, and open your heart to God.

> [2] My God, my God, why have you abandoned me? Why so far from my call for help, from my cries of anguish?
>
> [3] My God, I call by day, but you do not answer; by night, but I have no relief.
>
> [4] Yet you are enthroned as the Holy One; you are the glory of Israel.
>
> [5] In you our ancestors trusted; they trusted and you rescued them.
>
> [6] To you they cried out and they escaped; in you they trusted and were not disappointed.

Resting

Prayer is a relationship with God and we can learn much from our ordinary human relationships. God loved the world so much that he gave his only Son so that everyone who believes in him may have eternal life (cf. *John* 3:16). God's Son became part of our human story and now has ascended to the Father so that our human nature is inextricably connected with God, who desires to share with us eternal life, which is a participation in the divine life of the Blessed Trinity. Because of this, the relationship with God is not an exact parallel to the relationships we have with others. God sets about healing us and making us capable to receive eternal life and therefore to participate in the divine life. Our capacity is very small and it has to be increased little by little. Newborn babies cannot eat steak, and they have to go through various stages of growth before they can appreciate the finer things of life, so we also have to grow spiritually before we can receive what God wants to give us.

I think that we sometimes have a very low opinion of God and believe that the occasional nice feeling while we are praying is the summit of God's gifts. The word "contemplation" is often used in such a loose way that it is emptied of its real meaning. Some people, with very little background in their own Christian tradition, mix it with ill-digested pieces of Buddhism, Hinduism and whatever other "isms" they have picked up on the way. The result is a confused hodgepodge that nourishes no one. Each religious tradition has its own way of relating to God which cannot be separated from the background from which it has arisen. The Prophet Elijah in ancient Israel fought against idolatry among his own people. This was not a wholesale turning away from the God of Israel but was instead a creeping syncretism which merged two distinct religions into one amorphous blob. Elijah famously challenged the people on Mount Carmel: "How long will you hobble first on one leg and then the other? If the Lord is God, follow him. If Baal is god then follow him. The people never said a word." (*1 Kings* 18:21-22).

I seek to base myself on the Christian contemplation tradition which is enormously rich, and above all on my own Carmelite tradition, because that is what I know best. Contemplation, according to St. Teresa of Avila, is a kind of prayer which has moved beyond the beginnings. It prepares the human being for the most profound union with God. She distinguishes between momentary touches of contemplation, and the state of contemplation which she reserves for the higher reaches of mystical experience. The Lord seems to touch the soul of the one who prays in order to attract the individual into an ever deeper commitment. There can be passing experiences which we might put away into the memory drawer but do nothing about. A beautiful sunset might draw the mind to God, but it might not. However, these touches tend to be somewhat different in nature. According to Teresa there are two ways to go beyond the beginnings on our journey of prayer. The first way she calls "recollection" or "the prayer of recollection", and the other is "mystical contemplation" which cannot be conjured up by ourselves no matter what we do; it is entirely the work of God. Normally before entering on the path of contemplation we have to spend many years being faithful to the ordinary Christian virtues and to prayer, although God cannot be bound by rules.

For St. John of the Cross, contemplation runs from the moment an individual moves beyond the beginnings in prayer to the summit of Mount Carmel, which is the goal of the spiritual journey. John wrote because he was aware that there were many people in need of guidance and few suitable guides. For John, contemplation at the beginning was common and happens to many people. This kind of contemplation brings the more superficial aspects of the human being into conformity with God. The latter stages of contemplation where the more interior, deeper, aspects of the individual are reshaped by God, are rarer.[60]

When we read the Word of God and think about it, we are trying to extract the message that God has for us. This hopefully will touch our hearts and begin a dialogue with God that goes beyond our superficial thoughts. There comes a time when words subside and silence becomes an important part of the way we communicate with God. In the silence a space opens up for God to communicate directly with us. Silence can be difficult until we get used to it, and understand that it is in fact a surer means of communication than many words.

Spend some time in silence now, resting in the Word of God. There is no need for words or for holy thoughts. Let God mould you from within and excavate the infinite space needed to receive Him. Remain in silence however you can. Perhaps you might like to use the method of Centering Prayer that you can find described at the end of the Seventh Station.

What's Next?

Jesus soaked up the venom of those who insulted him and he remained faithful to the Father's will to the end. Each day we meet someone who is not exactly sweetness and light. Perhaps you could put your prayer into effect by not responding badly if someone crosses you.

---

60 'The Dark Night', 1.8.1, in K. Kavanaugh and O. Rodriguez, *The Collected Works of St. John of the Cross*, (Washington, D.C.: ICS Publications, 1991).

Jesus dies on the cross.
Ceramic by Adam Kossowski on the Rosary Way at Aylesford Priory, Kent,
marking the Fifth Sorrowful Mystery.

The Twelfth Station

JESUS DIES ON THE CROSS

Mark 15:33-37

Prayer

O Lord, your death brought life to the world. You entered fully into our human condition in order to transform it. Help me to remain faithful to you and to receive the gift of life that never ends. Amen.

Text

Read the piece of Scripture carefully to make sure that you have all the details of what happened in your mind. This text is taken from *The New Testament for Everyone*, translated by Tom Wright, the noted Scripture scholar.[61] He says that he has tried to stick closely to the original while respecting the fact that language evolves. Therefore what was a good translation in the past might not get over the meaning to a modern reader. He wanted to transmit the sense of excitement of the original.

> [33] At midday there was darkness over all the land until three in the afternoon. [34] At three o'clock Jesus shouted out in a powerful voice, '*Eloi, Eloi, lema sabachthani?*' Which means, 'My God, my God, why did you abandon me?' [35] When the bystanders heard it, some of them said, 'He's calling for Elijah!' [36] One of them ran and filled a sponge with sour wine, put it on a pole, and gave it to him to drink. 'Well then,' he declared, 'let's see If Elijah will come and take him down.' [37] But Jesus, with another loud shout, breathed his last.

Reading

Not much is said about the physical aspects of the death of Jesus. The interest is in the meaning of it, which is interpreted through the Scriptures. Mark actually says that darkness covered the earth from the sixth to the ninth hours, translated as from midday till three o'clock in the afternoon. All the Gospels except that of John mention the darkness at the same time. According to *Mark*

---

[61] Tom Wright, (trans.), *The New Testament for Everyone*, (London: S.P.C.K., 2011).

15:25, Jesus was crucified at the third hour (nine o'clock in the morning) and he died at the ninth hour (three o'clock). He hung on the cross for six hours. For the first three hours, no mercy has been shown to the Son of God by any human being, and now the whole earth grows dark until Jesus died. This is typical of the apocalyptic language often used in the Bible to describe events surrounding God's intervention in human affairs and no physical explanation need be sought. In the *Book of Wisdom* those who have been mocking the just one, doubting that he is a "son of God" exclaim: "We have strayed from the way of truth, and the light of justice did not shine for us, and the sun did not rise upon us" (5:6). There is also the darkness that marks the "day of the Lord", the time when God will visit the earth to punish sinners, according to the Old Testament outlook. A number of the prophets speak of darkness falling when God comes. The prophet Amos is interesting in this regard: "And on that day, says the Lord God, the sun shall set at midday, and the light shall be darkened on earth in the day time ... I will make them mourn as for an only son and bring their day to a bitter end." (8:9-10). The Prophet Joel, too, speaks of darkness on the day of the Lord (2:10).

"The land" over which the darkness fell might be the land of Israel, on whom judgement is passed, rather than the whole earth, but the latter translation is usually thought to be preferable. Raymond Brown believes that Mark's darkness means that while the mockers demanded of Jesus on the cross a sign (that he come down from the cross), God is giving them another sign as part of a judgement on the world. Throughout the story God has not been evident, but as Jesus drinks the cup that the Father has given him, divine intervention begins to be seen.[62] A little earlier in Mark's Gospel, Jesus speaks in these terms to describe the sorrows that would come upon Jerusalem before the coming of the Son of Man in glory. He tells of a time when the sun would be darkened (13:24).

Jesus' final words on the cross (his only words in Mark and *Matthew* 27:46-49) appear in three different forms in Mark/Matthew, Luke and John. In Mark and Matthew, Jesus lets out a loud cry and prays the opening words of *Psalm* 22. Prayers made with a loud cry are quite frequent in the Bible. In both Mark and Matthew, Jesus speaks the words of this psalm in what is probably Aramaic, the language that Jesus would have been brought up using. Apparently loud cries or screams were heard often from those who were being crucified. Three o'clock in the afternoon was the Jewish ritual time for the afternoon prayer.

---

62 Brown, *op. cit.*, Vol. II, p. 1035.

There is nothing that shows God is on the side of Jesus, and so the cry of Jesus seems appropriate. However, Jesus dies with a prayer on his lips. Jesus prophesied his own suffering and death several times throughout the Gospels as an important part of God's plan of salvation for the world (8:31; 9:31; 10:33). God exercises divine power only after the death of Jesus. At this point, in contrast to the prayer in Gethsemane when Jesus spoke to God as his "Abba, Father", now in the moment of dereliction, he speaks to God as "my God".

Regarding the offering of vinegary wine, there is an echo of the suffering just one in *Psalm* 69:22, "And they gave for my bread gall, and for my thirst they gave me vinegar to drink." This could have been a deliberate attempt to make fun of the dying man, or it might have been an act of mercy but that is not likely. There is a problem with what the bystanders understood Jesus to be saying. They thought that he was appealing to the Prophet Elijah to help him. The Aramaic of Jesus is unlikely to have sounded like that to the people at the foot of the cross. This suggests that Mark and his readers would not have understood that language.

The prophet Elijah was thought to be the helper of those in great need and was very prominent in popular expectations of what would happen when the messiah came. The last prediction in the Old Testament reads: "Behold I will send you Elijah the prophet before the day of the Lord comes, the great and terrible day." (*Malachi* 3:23 or 4:5 depending which Bible you have). Readers of Mark's Gospel know that Elijah has already come to prepare the way of the messiah (see *Mark* 9:11-13). Jesus had described earlier in his ministry the suffering that Elijah would undergo when he returned. He was speaking of John the Baptist who had been killed, so we know that Elijah is not coming to save Jesus. Therefore the offering of the vinegary wine to Jesus might have been an attempt to delay his imminent death in order to give time to the Prophet Elijah to show himself. This presumably was a sarcastic offer and so another way to make fun of the dying man.

Throughout the Gospel of Mark, there is a certain parallel between John the Baptist and Jesus. Like all the messengers sent by God to Israel, they are persecuted. The Prophet Elijah was persecuted in his time, and because of his mysterious end he was looked to as the one who would return to herald in the messiah.[63] Jesus understood John the Baptist to be the Elijah who had been promised (*Mark* 9:9-13).

---

63 The stories regarding the Prophet Elijah can be found in the two *Books of the Kings* in the Old Testament, from *1 Kings* 17 to *2 Kings* 1. See also my book *The Sound of Silence*, (Faversham & Rome: Saint Albert's Press & Edizioni Carmelitane, 2007) for a study of these stories using the traditional method of prayer called *Lectio Divina*.

JESUS DIES ON THE CROSS

From time to time medical people have written about the actual causes of Jesus' death without taking into account that the Gospel reports were never intended to be exact historical documents of what happened. A desire to know what actually happened at any moment in history is a fairly recent idea. The Gospels are documents of faith and they interpret the meaning of the death of Jesus with the religious background of the whole Bible and do not necessarily give us exact details.

Reflecting

Jesus experienced the loneliness of death. He died seemingly crushed by the forces of evil. Mark wanted those who would hear or read his Gospel to be aware of the price that Jesus paid for our salvation. It is remarkable that a man who was executed in the cruellest way possible should have inspired such devotion that countless people down the centuries would give up their lives rather than deny their faith in him. The faith of the first followers of Jesus was shaken when the one whom they apparently thought of as the Messiah promised by God to Israel did not at all fit into their ideas of what he should do. The group that was specially chosen by Jesus, known as the Twelve, is constantly shown in a bad light. These closest friends and disciples clearly had great difficulty in grasping what Jesus was on about. Finally he ended on the cross and they were naturally terrified in case the same thing happened to them. That was probably part of the reason for having him crucified, to make sure his followers got the message loud and clear and nip in the bud this movement.

This was not a very auspicious start to a movement that would, within three hundred years, replace all the old pagan gods that were central to the religion of the mighty Roman Empire. Not only that, but this Jesus movement went on to become the rock on which all western societies are founded. The fundamental values of these societies can be traced back to the message of this crucified Messiah. If people reject him, for how long will these fundamental values remain?

Through the Prophet Isaiah, God tells Israel: "My thoughts are not your thoughts, my ways not your ways" (*Isaiah* 55:8). God often does not do things the way we expect or want, but we are asked to trust that God's ways will actually turn out better than anything we might dream up. According to St. Paul, God turns everything to the good of those who love Him (*Romans* 8:28). That is easy to believe when things are going well, but when life takes a difficult turn it is not so easy. However God's love surrounds us at every moment and uses everything that happens for our growth. The challenge is to accept in faith that God is present even in difficult times, and to try to respond to what God seems to be asking of us.

The following questions are intended to help you enter more deeply into the mystery of the death of Christ on the cross. The purpose of reflecting on Scripture is particularly to find applications to our own lives, so what is God saying to you in this culmination of the story of the Passion of Jesus?

1. When things are very dark in your own life, to whom do you cry out and why?
2. When other people are going through dark times, how do you respond?
3. How could the will of God have been fulfilled in the death of Jesus?

The view of a passer-by

The Romans want everyone to see their so-called justice, so people going in and out of the city have to pass close by the place of execution. I didn't know the man, but no one deserves crucifixion. A lot of people seemed to hate him, but when he died everybody was silent.

The Romans killed him, but our own leaders obviously wanted him dead as well because he was a blasphemer. What people are saying about him now seems incredible. Surely God abandoned him? Was he a prophet? He would not be the first of our prophets to be killed. Our leaders will crush this new movement. I'm sure of that. I'm not going to get involved.

Responding

Prayer is a relationship with God, and in any relationship we do get involved. We can try to keep God at a distance or we can be vulnerable and allow God past our defences. We have spent some time reflecting on the Word of God and now comes the time to share with God not what we think but what we feel. What do you really want to say to God at this time in your life?

Perhaps this hymn quoted by St. Paul in his *Letter to the Philippians* (Chapter 2) might get you started:

JESUS DIES ON THE CROSS

⁵ Make your own the mind of Christ Jesus:

⁶ Who, being in the form of God, did not count equality with God something to be grasped.

⁷ But he emptied himself, taking the form of a slave, becoming as human beings are; and being in every way like a human being,

⁸ he was humbler yet, even to accepting death, death on a cross.

⁹ And for this God raised him high, and gave him the name which is above all other names;

¹⁰ so that all beings in the heavens, on earth and in the underworld, should bend the knee at the name of Jesus

¹¹ and that every tongue should acknowledge Jesus Christ as Lord, to the glory of God the Father.

Jesus died that you might have life, that is, a share of God's own eternal life. Take some time to speak to God from your heart.

Resting

According to St. Teresa of Avila, prayer is the way we enter into ourselves to meet God within. In her autobiography, Teresa comes up with perhaps the most famous analogy for prayer in the history of spirituality.[64] It is the analogy of the four waters irrigating the garden. The job of the one who is beginning to pray is to water the garden. The garden can be watered in four ways.

Firstly, we can walk to the well, let the bucket down, haul it up again, carry it to the garden, and pour the water over the plants. We must return to the well and repeat the operation as often as it takes to water the garden. This is very laborious and is the way of beginners who must learn to recollect themselves and to keep their attention on God. This can be difficult at first because there are innumerable distractions.

The second way of drawing water is much easier than the first. It is done by using a water wheel. You turn a handle and several buckets are filled. So you get more water with less work. The person at this stage sometimes experiences great consolations. Everything speaks to the individual of God and the whole of creation comes alive. At the same time the person normally becomes more able

---

64 St. Teresa of Avila, 'The Book of Her Life', 11-21, in *The Collected Works of St. Teresa of Avila*, Vol. 1, translated by Otilio Rodriguez & Kieran Kavanaugh, (Washington, D.C.: ICS Publications, 1976).

to exercise the normal Christian virtues. An increase of love, of practical love for others, is always a sign and fruit of progress on the spiritual journey. How we get on with other people is the test of the authenticity of any experience we may have had or think we have had in prayer. Saint Teresa calls the second way of watering the garden 'the prayer of quiet'. This is just a little spark of true love for the Lord and the spark must be carefully guarded. Prayer may flow easily at this stage. There is often no problem in becoming recollected. The person praying must not seek to have beautiful thoughts or make up great prayers but simply be happy to rest in the presence of God in faith. There usually is not a clear break between the first and second ways of prayer. They are intertwined and the passage can be almost imperceptible. The hard labour of using the imagination and concentrating on being recollected slowly becomes less and less. This is where prayer more obviously becomes less our work and more the work of God in us. It is sometimes difficult to understand that we need not do anything in prayer when the Lord has brought us into this second way. Prayer at this time is a being with God rather than thinking about Him.

The third way that the garden can be watered is by directing a stream through it. The gardener has very little to do here. The Lord invades the soul and the individual becomes profoundly influenced by the love of God. At this stage God Himself becomes the gardener and we become idle. We become much stronger in the basic Christian virtues. This way normally only comes after a long apprenticeship in the other ways of prayer, although God does not always follow this pattern.

The fourth way that the garden can be watered is when the Lord pours down His rain in abundance. At this stage the person does nothing. She simply enjoys the experience. God possesses the soul here but this possession is not yet definitive. During this prayer of union the person is not normally subject to distractions. There is certitude of being united with God and there is no possibility of doubt says Teresa. However, this state varies and the person can go back to an earlier stage of prayer. This prayer of union, as described in her autobiography, is only the beginning of union, and in her other works she describes its further stages.

Teresa explained why we do not learn to love God perfectly in a short time. She said that we think "we are giving all to God, whereas the truth of the matter is that we are paying God the rent or giving Him the fruits and keeping for ourselves the ownership and the root" (*Life* 11.2). God wants ALL so that He can transform us. We can so easily hand over some little part of ourselves, believing that we are giving all, and then we take back little by little what we did give. Teresa gives the example of abandoning all thoughts of our own importance: "No sooner is some little point of etiquette concerning our status brought up than we forget that we have already offered it to God; and we desire to take it right back out of His hands, so to speak, after having made Him, as it seemed, the Lord of our wills" (*Life* 11.2).

Jesus surrendered his life into the hands of the Father. He had always sought to be obedient to the Father's will and it had brought him to death on the cross. At this point he rested after his life's work was done. Now spend some time simply resting in the presence of God, not trying to think holy thoughts or say prayers, but simply to be silent. Let God irrigate the ground of your heart. You may find a method like Centering Prayer (as described in earlier Stations) useful at this time.

What's Next?

I have said above that the test of the authenticity of our prayer is how we treat other people. There are some people to whom we are naturally more attracted and it is somewhat easier to treat these more kindly than others. Jesus did equate how we treat the ones we are not attracted to with how we treat him (*Matthew* 25:31-46) and also he told us that we are to love even our enemies and those who persecute us (*Matthew* 5:43-44; *Luke* 6:27-35). Try to bring God's love into the life of someone else simply by treating them with kindness and do not expect any thanks.

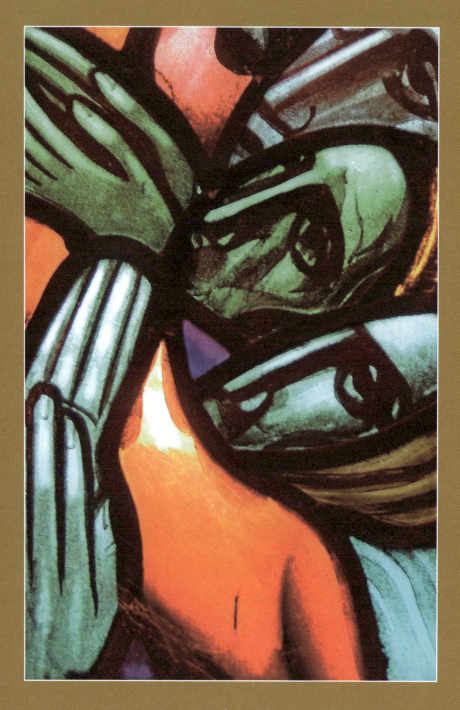

*Faces of anguish.
Window by Richard Joseph King
at the National Shrine of St. Jude, Faversham.*

The Thirteenth Station

REACTION TO THE DEATH OF JESUS

Mark 15:38-41

Prayer

Father, you sent your Son to bring Good News to the world. At the end, as he died on the cross, a new era of grace and reconciliation opened for the human race. Help me, like the centurion, to recognise him in the face of suffering humanity, and to wait with the women for the resurrection that is to come. Amen.

Text

Read the piece of Scripture below in order to grasp all the facts. The translation used is from the *World English Bible* which is based on *The American Standard Version*, first published in 1901.[65]

> [38] The veil of the temple was torn in two from the top to the bottom. [39] When the centurion, who stood by opposite him, saw that he cried out like this and breathed his last, he said, "Truly this man was the Son of God!" [40] There were also women watching from afar, among whom were both Mary Magdalene, and Mary the mother of James the less and of Joses, and Salome; [41] who, when he was in Galilee, followed him, and served him; and many other women who came up with him to Jerusalem.

Reading

Several times before this point Mark has referred to the "temple", which was the symbol of God's presence in the midst of the chosen people. In 14:58 some witnesses gave false evidence against Jesus that he would destroy the temple made by hand and within three days build another not made by hand. Also as Jesus hung on the cross, those who passed by mocked him referring to this evidence (15:29). Jesus is now vindicated. Tearing the veil somehow destroys the sanctuary and God is to be understood as the One who caused the tearing of

---

[65] *The World English Bible*, (Rainbow Missions, 2000). This is a modern version of the Bible in the public domain (not subject to copyright) and can be found on the internet at www.ebible.org

REACTION TO THE DEATH OF JESUS

the veil. At the beginning of the public ministry, God tears open the heavens to declare to Jesus: "You are my Son, the Beloved; my favour rests on you" (1:10-11). When God tears the veil of the Temple, the centurion recognises Jesus as God's Son (15:39). The destruction of the Temple is the divine response to the death of Jesus declaring that God has not forsaken him, as some supposed, and that it is the chief priests and scribes who have done great evil.

There were two curtains in the Temple. There was the outer curtain that was very ornate with signs of the zodiac on it. There was also an inner curtain that separated the Holy of Holies. Mark does not specify which curtain he intends and it is not entirely clear exactly what he wanted to say here. The curtain or veil was a way of marking the distinction between the sacred and the profane, and so when it was torn in two the holy character of the place was destroyed. The old covenant that bound God to Israel is at an end, and a new one has taken its place. In Jewish law only the high priest entered the Holy of Holies once each year. Now it is open to all through Jesus. Even the pagans can now go to God through faith in Jesus, the crucified messiah. The curtain is destroyed in a way that it cannot be repaired, and so Mark understood that with the death of Christ the Temple had been destroyed forever. Jesus had been accused of declaring that he would replace the Temple with another sanctuary not made with human hands (14:58; 15:29). In the year 70 A.D. the Romans physically destroyed the Temple in Jerusalem and removed every trace of it. Those who heard this Gospel after that date must have connected the act of the Romans with the prophecy of the tearing of the sanctuary curtain. It is unlikely that any of the hearers or readers had ever seen the Temple or had more than a very basic idea of what the sanctuary curtain was for.

The three Synoptic Gospels report the same phenomenon, and it seems that Luke and Matthew copied what Mark wrote. Looking at the whole of Mark's Gospel we can see how this simple scene has a part to play in the bigger picture. The heavens are torn open at the beginning of Jesus' public ministry to identify him as God's beloved Son. The tearing of the sanctuary veil at the end of his ministry displays God's anger at the authorities in Jerusalem for not having listened to him. The next verse about the centurion identifying Jesus as God's Son shows that the pagans will listen to the Good News.

It seems that the centurion, the Roman officer presumably in charge of the crucifixion detail, was responding to the fact that Jesus had died with the name of God on his lips and that the tearing of the curtain of the sanctuary showed that God had not abandoned the crucified man. This was a divine response to the death of Jesus and to those who mocked him. It is unlikely that the centurion could have physically seen whether the Temple veil had been torn, but such an objection would be to impose a twenty-first-century objection to a first-century text where considerations of historical exactitude would not be so important. Mark is interested in the meaning of Jesus' death more than the precise details that would be necessary in a court of law.

Some people say that the centurion did not state that Jesus was "the" Son of God but merely "a" son of God. However, it seems that Mark does want us to understand the phrase in its stronger sense. Until this point no human being has recognised Jesus, although a demon has (1:24; 3:11; 5:7). The first words of Mark's Gospel are, "The beginning of the Good News about Jesus Christ, Son of God" (1:1). God recognises Jesus as "Beloved Son" at the baptism of Jesus, and now at the end we see the Good News being accepted by the pagans in the person of the Roman centurion who understands that Jesus is Son of God.

Some writers believe that all the centurion was saying was that Jesus was a very good man. This is most unlikely for all sorts of reasons. At his trial, the high priest formally asked Jesus whether he was "the Son of the Blessed One", a euphemism for God, since the Jewish people avoided using the sacred name. Jesus accepted this title, and the leaders found this answer blasphemous. Now the centurion confirms that truth was in fact on the side of Jesus. If Mark is intending to report the scene as it happened, it is impossible to know what a Roman centurion would have meant at the time. We do not even know what language he would have spoken. What is important is to have an idea of what Mark wanted to get across to his first readers or hearers about thirty or forty years after the scene. At that time the centurion would have represented the Gentile world as well as the Roman Empire which ruled the earth. The chief priests and scribes demanded that Jesus come down from the cross so that they might see and believe in him as the Messiah. Now a Gentile and Roman officer has indeed seen and believed. He has recognised in the suffering and dead Jesus the one who was indeed Son of God.

Earlier in the Gospel of Mark, Jesus says that the Good News must be proclaimed to all the nations (13:10). The statement of the centurion is the beginning of the fulfilment of Jesus' desire or prophecy. The centurion is the first human being in Mark's Gospel to recognise Jesus as Son of God and so he represents all the pagans who would put their faith in Christ and follow him.

The second response to the death of Jesus comes from the silent presence of a group of women, among whom were three named individuals. Perhaps this whole group, or perhaps only the three, had followed Jesus for some time.

REACTION TO THE DEATH OF JESUS

They were looking on from a distance. This is perhaps a reference to *Psalm* 38:11, which says that "even the dearest keep their distance". Mark had never mentioned that women were in the habit of following Jesus, and so he supplies this detail now, telling us that they used to minister to him when he was in Galilee. The impression is that none of the women was native to Jerusalem. The first to be mentioned is Mary Magdalene, that is, Mary from the town of Magdala on the shore of the Sea of Galilee. She is not to be confused with another great friend of Jesus, Mary of Bethany, and not with the sinful woman in Luke's Gospel (7:36-50). Luke does say that Jesus had banished seven demons from Mary of Magdala (*Luke* 8:2) and so it is often assumed that she was a great sinner, but this could have referred to some illness. Then we have Mary, the mother of James the younger (or the small one) and Joses. Finally we have Salome, which was a common name in Palestine at the time. Mark also mentions that many other women were in the habit of following Jesus during his public ministry.

It is a mistake to read modern Church issues into this scene of the women looking on as Jesus dies. All those who are close to Christ, family and disciples, fall short according to Mark, during his lifetime. The first readers and hearers of Mark's Gospel would have been consoled by his portrayal of all the disciples. Even those who failed would be welcomed back and perhaps there is a warning to those who had not denied Jesus in the various persecutions that arose only because they had kept their distance, that they had not been covered in glory either.

Reflecting

Were the enemies of Jesus happy that they had finally brought him down and silenced him? He had told many stories to the simple people of Galilee that suggested the religious leaders were not doing God's will and that he had some special understanding of what God wanted. Even some of the "sophisticated" people in Jerusalem began to be captivated by his teaching. All sorts of rumours were going around about who Jesus was. Some ideas were absurd, and others would have been dangerous if they had been picked up by the Romans and misinterpreted.

In the Passion story, it is clear that Jesus was mocked even on the cross. However, Mark and the other evangelists want to stress with the reading we had in this Station what is God's response to the death of His Son. They also open up the story of Israel's messiah to the whole world. When the Gospels were written, a lot of non-Jews had responded very positively to the preaching about the death and resurrection of Jesus, and many had come to believe in him. This was a problem to the first Jewish followers of Jesus. We hear in *The Acts of the Apostles* how the first Christians had to work out with some difficulty how non-Jews could be accepted in their midst. Saint Paul fought long and hard for the full acceptance of gentiles into the Church. In the piece of Scripture for this Station, we hear the famous words of the centurion, who represents the gentile world and the Roman Empire. It is clear that in the tearing of the veil plus the words of this soldier we are intended to understand that the God of Israel can no longer be confined but that all races are welcome to the feast in the Kingdom of God.

The women who looked on from a distance can give some comfort that Jesus was not totally alone in Mark's account of the Passion. At least he had some friends, although they were far off. They had stayed with him during his ministry in Galilee and they had not abandoned him at the end.

The whole point of the Gospels was to announce the Good News from God about Jesus. His death seemed like a disaster to his friends and a triumph for the enemies of Jesus, but the Gospels make it clear that, in the words of St. Paul, "where sin abounded, grace abounded even more" (*Romans* 5:20). Not even death could destroy the life that Jesus came to bring into the world. The Father wanted simply to share the divine life with the whole of creation, but when it was rejected so emphatically by nailing the Son of God to the cross, the death of Jesus became the opportunity to flood the world with a new outpouring of grace. By dying, he destroyed our death and opened wide the gates into the Kingdom of the Father for all people to enter. In this completely unforeseen development, the mission of the Chosen People had been fulfilled in and through one man.

God's plan of salvation had always required a faithful Israelite to fulfil it. In Jesus, God provided such a one. Jesus has done what Israel as a whole was called to do. Jesus showed us the way out of the impasse of sin and death, and opens the way through which everyone who wishes will receive eternal life.

Perhaps some of the following questions might help you to see more clearly the relevance of the death of Jesus to your own life at present. Take your time and ponder your answer before God.

1. What is the role of God's chosen people today?
2. In the Church there are people of every race, language and way of life. Who would you exclude from salvation?
3. What does it mean for you that Jesus, who was crucified, is the Son of God?

REACTION TO THE DEATH OF JESUS

The story of a carpenter

Everybody has to make a living. I prefer to make other things but 'needs must'. I make all the crosses for the Romans. At least they pay me. I actually take a bit of trouble making them, you know. I realise what they are going to be used for. A man is going to die on one of my crosses and no matter what he has done, the least he deserves is a well-made cross.

They say he was a blasphemer. I don't know anything about that. I keep out of trouble and make what I'm asked to. Somebody told me that he is supposed to be alive now. Look, the Romans don't make mistakes. When they crucify someone, he's dead, know what I mean? There's a funny atmosphere around Jerusalem. I don't know how he could be alive. I hope they don't blame me. There was nothing wrong with my cross.

Responding

The Roman centurion looked upon the dead Jesus and he saw more than a dead man. He saw the Son of God. Only one who can accept that paradox can make the Christian profession of faith. "God's foolishness is wiser than human wisdom, and God's weakness is stronger than human strength" (*1 Corinthians 1:22-25*). Looking on the awful scene are some followers of Jesus. The brave men have all fled, but some women stay there.

Imagine you are with those women. What do you see? What is your response? To get you started, perhaps the following quote from the Prophet Isaiah (*Isaiah 48*) might help:

> ⁶ Now I am going to reveal new things to you, secrets that you do not know; ⁷ they have just been created, not long ago, and until today you have heard nothing about them, so that you cannot say, 'Yes, I knew about this.'

Now pour out your heart to God. Take whatever time you need.

Resting

The central theme of the writings of St. Teresa is the attachment to the person of Christ through prayer. She viewed prayer as the privileged means of communication with God. There are, of course, many ways of prayer. The first way is generally 'vocal prayer' when we speak to God aloud. This can be done in private or together with other people. When we come together for the celebration of Morning and Evening Prayer and the Mass, we are praying the prayer of the whole Church. Christ is Our High Priest and he is forever mediating between us and the Father. His prayer is always ascending before the throne of grace. We are members of the Body of Christ, and when the Church comes together to pray we share in the unending prayer of Christ. This prayer is the greatest and highest prayer of all.

However, Jesus, echoing God's complaints in the Old Testament, condemned the attitude of the Pharisees whose lips proclaimed God but whose hearts were far from Him (*Mark* 7:6; *Matthew* 15:8). In Teresa's day there were many false visionaries. Some people, who nowadays would be treated for mental illness, were popularly thought to be saints and greatly favoured by God. They could easily lead people astray. When Teresa started having visions, she feared that she might be deluded and even that she could be possessed by the devil. She was quick to explain everything to confessors and spiritual directors who eventually managed to put her at ease. What she experienced was not from the devil but from God. Teresa wrote her autobiography at the command of her confessors so that they could judge the authenticity of her experiences.

Because of the false visionaries who were going around, some believed that people should normally limit themselves to the recitation of the *Our Father* and *Hail Mary* and not try anything advanced for fear that they might become deluded! Many good spiritual books in Spanish were banned because it was thought that they might tempt simple people to things beyond them.

The thrust of all Teresa's writings is about 'mental prayer' as she calls it. She defines mental prayer as "nothing but friendly intercourse and frequent solitary converse with Him who we know loves us" (*Life* 8.5). She accepts the counsel that the recitation of the *Our Father* and the *Hail Mary* are quite sufficient, but she adds that it would be an insult to God to pray to Him without at least thinking of what we are saying. Thinking of what we are saying to God is the beginning of mental prayer. A large part of one of her books, *The Way of Perfection*, is a meditation on the *Our Father* in which she draws out some of the riches of this prayer.[66] Each little phrase in the Lord's Prayer is a treasure. She gives thanks to God that He is pleased to call Himself "Our Father"; she gives thanks to Christ that he took on our condition and became our brother. All of us are called to be children of God and this gives us an equal rank which makes any human distinctions between classes of people utterly ridiculous. Then we are reminded that Our Father is in heaven. Teresa reminds her readers also of the truth that God is everywhere, and she says that wherever God is, there is heaven too. Therefore, she writes:

> *Do you suppose it is of little importance that a soul which is often distracted should come to understand this truth and to find that, in order to speak to its Eternal Father and to take its delight in Him, it has no need to go to Heaven or to speak in a loud voice? However quietly we speak, He is so near that He will hear us: we need no wings to go in search of Him but have only to find a place where we can be alone and look upon Him present within us. (Way 28.2)*

According to Teresa, mental prayer has little or nothing to do with keeping the lips closed (*Way* 22.1). Mental prayer begins when we become aware of the God who dwells within us and speak to Him in the depths of our hearts. The whole of the Christian life, as St. Teresa sees it, is a growing relationship with God through Christ who dwells within us by the power of the Holy Spirit. Prayer is the way we enter into ourselves to meet God within.

What we need is a desire to pray and then actually to begin. The best way to learn to pray is to pray. Reading innumerable books about prayer will not help us unless we actually pray. Saint Augustine said that our hearts are restless until they find their rest in God. He put into words what is a universal phenomenon. We are searching for something more. None of us is totally happy at all times. If we go a bit deeper, we discover that we are not searching for something but Someone. We are being drawn by God into a life of union with Him.

Jesus said to the Samaritan woman at the well, "If you but knew the gift of God and who it is that is saying to you: Give me a drink – you would have been the one to ask, and he would have given you living water" (*John* 4:10). Prayer, first of all, is a response of gratitude and adoration for what God is offering us, that is, His love is always there at the very depth of our being keeping us in existence. Prayer then is a dialogue of love between Creator and creature. It has its beginnings not in our desire to find God because we could not seek Him

---

66 St. Teresa of Avila, 'The Way of Perfection', in *The Collected Works of St. Teresa of Avila*, Volume 2, translated by Otilio Rodriguez & Kieran Kavanaugh, (Washington, D.C.: ICS Publications, 1980).

unless God had planted this desire within us. It has its beginnings in God who addresses His word to us.

Teresa discovered a book which helped her enter into herself and gave her a method of prayer. Nowadays various prayer methods are suggested. Teresa's method was very simply to picture Christ in some aspect of his life and talk to him or simply to be with him. When I say "picture Christ", I do not mean that she conjured up a mental image. She said that she had little imagination for that. No, in faith she would simply believe that Christ was within her, for example hanging on the cross, and she would gaze at him with the eyes of faith and speak to him as her greatest friend.

Most modern methods will give instruction on having a good posture and various other preliminaries to prayer. God, however, cannot be grasped by the use of any method of prayer, no matter how clever. He can only be grasped by love. God gives Himself to whom He wishes when He wishes. Our part is to prepare ourselves to receive this great gift of God Himself. Of course God is already within us, so perhaps it would be better to say that prayer is a growing awareness in love of the God who already dwells within us. By our prayer we show that we want to take seriously this relationship and that we are prepared to wait patiently until God chooses to invite us further. Any method of prayer that helps us wait on God can help us. The method of 'Centering Prayer', outlined in the Seventh Station of this book, is a prayer of consent to God's presence and action in our lives. If God wants us to wait, so be it. God does not play games with us, and so the feeling of just waiting will actually be for our benefit, though we might not be able to discern the reason immediately. It is better to pray with no expectations.

In *The Way of Perfection*, Teresa says that prayer cannot be accompanied by self-indulgence. She lays down three attitudes which are vital for true prayer: love of neighbour; detachment from earthly things; and humility. We see from this that it is not enough to have a good method of prayer, but the way we live is vital. The way to test whether we are growing spiritually is not to be always looking at how we pray and what we feel at prayer, but to look at our daily lives. Are we growing in love for those around us? Are we becoming less possessive and grasping of material goods? Are we growing in true humility, that is, a true knowledge of ourselves?

How about spending some time in silence now just waiting for God, consenting to whatever it is God desires to do within you? Twenty minutes is a normal period of time for this phase, but more is not bad.

REACTION TO THE DEATH OF JESUS

What's Next?

Read again the Scripture text we have been using for this station, *Mark* 15:38-41. It is about the reactions to the death of Jesus. What is your reaction? How are you going to make sure that you honour all that Jesus did by putting into practice what he taught? It does not have to be a grand gesture. Remember the widow's mite (*Mark* 12:41-44). The woman who put a tiny amount into the Temple coffers gave more than all the rich people with their magnificent offerings.

Jesus is laid in the tomb.
Fourteenth Station in the Relic Chapel at Aylesford Priory.
Ceramic by Adam Kossowski.

The Fourteenth Station

THE BURIAL OF JESUS

Mark 15:42-47

Prayer

O Lord, the funeral had to be quick with no time for speeches. They buried you in a borrowed grave with a few followers looking on. Everything had started with so much promise but you would not compromise the mission you had received from the Father and this brought you to death on a cross. Lord, you know that so many people in our own day "disappear" or are buried in unmarked graves. Sustain our hope that death is not the end and that the darkness of the grave will be flooded by the light of new life that only you can give. Amen.

Text

Read the following piece of Scripture with care, noting all the different facts that make up the story. This translation is taken from *The New American Standard Bible* (*NASB*).[67] This is an updated version of the first one, which was produced in 1960.

> [42] When evening had already come, because it was the preparation day, that is, the day before the Sabbath, [43] Joseph of Arimathea came, a prominent member of the Council, who himself was waiting for the kingdom of God; and he gathered up courage and went in before Pilate, and asked for the body of Jesus. [44] Pilate wondered if He was dead by this time, and summoning the centurion, he questioned him as to whether He was already dead. [45] And ascertaining this from the centurion, he granted the body to Joseph. [46] Joseph bought a linen cloth, took Him down, wrapped Him in the linen cloth and laid Him in a tomb which had been hewn out in the rock; and he rolled a stone against the entrance of the tomb. [47] Mary Magdalene and Mary the *mother* of Joses were looking on *to see* where He was laid.

---

[67] Scripture taken from the *New American Standard Bible*, Copyright © 1960-1995 The Lockman Foundation. Used by permission.

THE BURIAL OF JESUS

Reading

All the Gospels agree on the fact that Jesus was buried in a tomb which was distinguishable from others and that there were witnesses to this fact. It seems clear that Matthew and Luke base their accounts of this scene on what Mark gives us here. According to Jewish law, sunset marks the beginning of a new day. The last indication of time is at 3 p.m. when Jesus died. Therefore it is probable that when Mark says evening had come, he is intending somewhere between 3 p.m. and sunset. All the actions that are involved before Jesus was placed in the tomb are unlikely to have taken less than two hours, and so the burial was probably around 5 p.m. Mark tells his readers that it was the preparation day and then goes to the trouble of explaining what he means, "that is, the day before the Sabbath." This is a little indication, along with many others throughout the Gospel, that Mark does not expect his readers to know firsthand all the details of Judaism.

All the Gospels mention Joseph of Arimathea for the first time at this point. Although Mark had blamed all the members of the Sanhedrin previously for their condemnation of Jesus, he points out that this Joseph was different. It is not necessary to believe that Joseph was actually a disciple of Jesus, at least at the time that Jesus died, from the information that Mark gives us. Matthew (27:57) and John (19:38) say that he was a disciple, while Luke, like Mark, tells us that he was waiting for the Kingdom of God (23:51).

Of course Jesus had proclaimed from the beginning of his ministry that he was the bearer of Good News in that the Kingdom of God had come. Through his miracles and teaching he proclaimed this same reality. The fact that Joseph was waiting for the Kingdom of God might mean that he was a good man who was awaiting God's intervention in history but had not yet recognised the presence of God in Jesus.

Why would someone who was not a disciple of Jesus pluck up his courage to go before Pilate and request the body of a crucified blasphemer for burial? The answer to this could very well be that Joseph was a good Jew and he wanted to obey the law of God by making sure that the body did not hang on the cross overnight. In the *Book of Deuteronomy* it states: "If a man guilty of a capital offence is to be put to death, and you hang him from a tree, his body must not remain on the tree overnight; you must bury him the same day, since anyone hanged is a curse of God, and you must not bring pollution on the soil which the Lord your God is giving you as your heritage" (21:22-23). Normally the Romans left the bodies of the crucified to rot but it seems they bowed to

Jewish customs. It is more likely that Pilate would concede to the request from a member of the Sanhedrin who had handed Jesus over for condemnation than from a disciple of the dead man.

According to the story as reported in Mark's Gospel, Pilate wondered if Jesus were already dead. Jesus had been hanging on the cross for six hours. People lasted for varying lengths of time on the cross and much would depend on the treatment they had received previously as well as how they had been crucified. Therefore it would have been a normal question to ask. Probably Mark has this in his Gospel story because there were tales from opponents that Jesus had not in fact died and so Mark wants to stress the reality of Jesus' death. After the centurion's assurance, Pilate allows the body of Jesus to be taken down from the cross and given to Joseph of Arimathea for burial. Actually Mark says "the corpse" to emphasise that Jesus was really dead with no room for doubt. The only other time that Mark uses this word is when John the Baptist was killed (6:29). This is another instance of linking the destinies of Jesus and John the Baptist. The other Gospels prefer the less stark word "body".

Little is said about the burial which would suggest that it was done in a hurry and without frills. The traditional site of the burial is within a few yards of the traditional place of execution. The two women are mentioned as witnesses. No mention is made of washing the body or anointing it. Jewish law forbade giving the body of a man condemned by the Jewish courts an honourable burial. It is not clear what would have marked an honourable from a dishonourable burial in the time of Jesus. Presumably for an honourable burial, the most basic service would be to wash the body and this would have applied particularly to a crucified man as he would have been covered in blood. None of the Gospels mention that the body was washed. No customary lamentation is recorded in the case of Jesus. There is, however, quite a difference on this point between Mark, basically followed by the other two Synoptic Gospels, and John. While Mark does not seem to envisage an honourable burial, John's version does. However, the body of Jesus could have been thrown into a common grave so presumably Joseph of Arimathea, even if he was not a disciple, had at least some respect for the crucified preacher.

It is not clear what kind of linen cloth Joseph bought for the burial. Mark says that the body of Jesus was tied up in a linen cloth, which apparently was the absolute minimum one would do for burial. This makes sense if Joseph of Arimathea was not a disciple of Christ at the time of the crucifixion and was burying the body out of a sense of duty to the Jewish law. He might very well have done this for anyone. Remember the First Station where Jesus understood that what the woman had done in pouring oil over him was to anoint his body before burial (*Mark* 14:8) because he knew that this would not be done when he was actually being buried.

Next Joseph, or his servants perhaps, roll a stone against the door of the tomb. These tombs, cut into the rock, were quite common around Jerusalem and several examples can be seen to this day. Matthew adds the interesting little detail in his Gospel that the tomb belonged to Joseph (*Matthew* 27:60). Tombs were intended to hold a number of bodies, so Matthew, Luke and John tell us that the tomb was new and so far unused, although Mark does not mention this. The typical tomb had a short entrance leading to one or more burial chambers. The stones, usually square or rectangular, were very large and difficult to move.

Having closed the tomb, Mark then turns our attention to the presence of the two Marys. The first, Mary Magdalene, was one of the witnesses to the crucifixion "from a distance" and she also went to the tomb to anoint the body of Jesus on the Sunday morning. The second woman is presumably the same as the one who witnessed the death of Jesus, only this time she is identified in a shorthand form. The same is probably true at the empty tomb, although there she is identified in another way. Very confusing! Therefore they observe Jesus die, they watch the burial, and they are witnesses to the resurrection. We are not told that the women were involved in any way in the burial of Jesus beyond seeing where he was buried.

Reflecting

Jesus was definitely dead and now was buried. A funeral is always the end. It is important to have a funeral so that those who were close can say goodbye. Funeral rites differ according to the religion of the deceased. The ones that I find the saddest are those where the family do not want a mention of God or where only those who absolutely have to be there attend with no member of family or friend to mark the end of a human life.

This was a hurried affair to get the tomb sealed before the Sabbath began. Everything was done in a hurry. The time for prayers and the other customary rites could come when the Sabbath was over. What a way to end the life of someone who had proclaimed that the Kingdom of God was near. So many people had hoped in him and now it was finished.

Joseph of Arimathea, whether he had been a disciple of Jesus or not, was a good man. He wanted to obey God's Law which did not allow the body of a condemned man to hang overnight. Other people did not seem to care, but he did, and the two women did also. They noted the place where Jesus was buried, presumably intending to return when the Sabbath was over to pay their last respects to the one whom they had followed from Galilee.

No doubt you have been to the funeral of someone close. Did the ceremony help you in your grieving or do you still need to let go of something? Have you forgiven what needs to be forgiven? Are you still angry about something? Are you angry that your loved one left you alone? Talk to God about it.

As well as those questions perhaps the following might help you to see how the story of Jesus being buried might have some relevance for your life.

1. Why do you think Joseph of Arimathea went to the trouble of burying Jesus? What would you have done?
2. The women stayed close up to the very end. Are you willing to stay close to Jesus in good and bad times?

Mary Magdalene's account

It all happened so quickly. Everything was wonderful when he began his ministry. I heard about him, that he was a great preacher and a healer. I must admit that it was the healing bit I was most interested in then. My health was not good at all and he healed me, but he did much more. He looked at me and I knew that I was known and loved for who I am in that one look.

I started following him from then on. I left everything behind. There were a few of us women but he treated us as equals and each one was an individual. I really loved him and I wanted to do everything I could to support him in his mission. He spoke so beautifully and so simply about God. The one I liked best was when he said that God was like a woman who loses a precious coin and she sweeps out the whole house till she finds it. Then she invites all her neighbours to celebrate with her! I've done that myself.

Everybody loved him. Well, not everybody. There were some grumblers from the beginning but then he began to make enemies just by speaking the truth. Some people couldn't grasp that what he was offering was good news from God. I was frightened when he spoke about what was going to happen to him, but I was determined to stay with him. Then we set out for Jerusalem and the feast. Things

> went badly very quickly. He was arrested and the brave men ran away. Peter followed him to the place where he was being tried. He told me everything. I admire Peter for telling the truth even though it didn't show him up in a good light.
>
> What happened then was too painful to talk about. They crucified him. We were all frightened but some of us stayed. We got as close as we dared and we hoped that he would know that we were near. We watched him die. He came to give us life and we killed him! We watched as he was taken down from the cross lifeless, and we watched where that kind man, Joseph of Arimathea, buried him.
>
> I have a lot more to say but I can't at the moment. I will tell the whole story soon.

Responding

Read the story of the burial of Jesus again slowly. Is there anything in particular that stands out for you? Perhaps the story raises memories of the deaths of people you have loved and lost. Now is the time to let your heart speak to the heart of God.

We are followers of Christ who died and rose again from the dead, so we are not just looking back in admiration at the life of a dead hero; we are following Christ in faith. Perhaps the following prayer might help you to begin your dialogue of the heart. It is from Eucharistic Prayer III used at Mass, particularly to remember someone who has died:

> Remember your servant whom you have called from this world to yourself. Grant that he (she), who was united with your Son in a death like his, may also be one with him in his Resurrection, when from the earth he will raise up in the flesh those who have died and transform our lowly body after the pattern of his own glorious body. To our departed brothers and sisters, too, and to all who were pleasing to you at their passing from this life, give kind admittance to your kingdom. There we hope to enjoy forever the fullness of your glory, when you will wipe away every tear from our eyes.
>
> For seeing you, our God, as you are, we shall be like you for all the ages and praise you without end, through Christ our Lord, through whom you bestow on the world all that is good.

Resting

We have followed Jesus on this way of the cross and here we watch him being buried. Saint Teresa was aware that in her own day some people, who thought themselves to be advanced on the spiritual journey, advised that one must leave Jesus behind in order to ascend to a less material concept of divinity. However, she eventually came to realise that these people were profoundly wrong, and that one never moved beyond Jesus because he is the one through whom we come to the Father and from whom we receive the Spirit.

Christian prayer is a relationship with God in and through Jesus Christ, and like any relationship it has its times and seasons. There are times when we need to talk, other times when we need to have a heart-to-heart, and there are also times when it is right simply to be with the other in a loving silence. John of the Cross writes of the passage into contemplation when the individual simply desires to be alone in loving awareness of God in interior peace and quiet without actively thinking or talking.[68] He counsels a "very deep and delicate listening" in order to receive the loving knowledge of God which God seeks to impart at this time. The individual must not lean on any thought or method that "would impede and disquiet them and make noise in the profound silence of their senses and their spirit".[69] This is not a state that can be brought on just by willing it, much less simply because we use a particular method of prayer. Any method of Christian prayer is designed to enkindle love for God in the depths of the individual. It can take some time to get a decent fire going, but once it has taken hold all that is required is to make sure it does not go out.

Saint Teresa points out that this kind of deep resting in God does produce good effects. The person gradually discovers a greater degree of self control and begins to experience freedom from some of the things that dominated her previously. This is a freedom from in order to be free to. There is a gradual growth in the basic Christian virtues of faith, hope and charity. Saint John of the Cross wrote much about the 'dark night', which is an experience or set of experiences by means of which these fundamental virtues find their root in God alone and not in any human reasoning: "Faith and love are like the blind man's guides. They will lead you along a path unknown to you, to the place where God is hidden."[70]

---

[68] cf. 'Ascent of Mount Carmel', Bk. II, 13, 4, in *The Collected Works of St. John of the Cross, op. cit.*
[69] cf. 'Living Flame of Love', 3, 34, in *The Collected Works of St. John of the Cross, op. cit.*
[70] 'The Spiritual Canticle', I, 11, in *The Collected Works of St. John of the Cross, op. cit.*

Are you growing in faith, hope and love? Ask the Lord to lead you "to the place where God is hidden". Spend some time in silence, which can be more eloquent than many words.

What's Next?

The disciples of Jesus must have been in utter confusion after his death and burial. They had followed him with so much hope but often they did not really grasp what he was talking about. It is only the light of the resurrection and the outpouring of the Holy Spirit that would bring them a profound understanding of who Jesus is and that they were to carry on his mission until the end of time.

Each of us has a particular vocation, a particular part to play in the mission of Jesus. You might not be fully aware of what God is calling you to do, but you can exercise your faith, your hope and your love today.

*The women encounter the angel at the empty tomb.
Fifteenth Station in the Relic Chapel at Aylesford Priory.
Ceramic by Adam Kossowski.*

THE FIFTEENTH STATION

THE EMPTY TOMB

Mark 16:1-8

Prayer

O God, I have followed your Son in prayer through his passion and death, and now to the joy of the resurrection. Help me to know the presence of the Risen Christ with me in all the joys and sorrows of life. Through Christ Our Lord. Amen.

Text

Read the Scripture for this last Station carefully to make sure you have all the facts. The translation this time comes from *The Revised English Bible*.[71] This is a revision of the *New English Bible* and care has been taken to ensure the style of English used is fluent and of appropriate dignity for liturgical use, while maintaining intelligibility for a wide range of ages and backgrounds.

> [1] When the sabbath was over, Mary of Magdala, Mary the mother of James, and Salome bought aromatic oils, intending to go and anoint him; [2] and very early on the first day of the week, just after sunrise, they came to the tomb. [3] They were wondering among themselves who would roll away the stone for them from the entrance to the tomb, [4] when they looked up and saw that the stone, huge as it was, had been rolled back already. [5] They went into the tomb, where they saw a young man sitting on the right-hand side, wearing a white robe; and they were dumbfounded. [6] But he said to them, 'Do not be alarmed; you are looking for Jesus of Nazareth, who was crucified. He has been raised; he is not here. Look, there is the place where they laid him. [7] But go and say to his disciples and to Peter: "He is going ahead of you into Galilee: there you will see him, as he told you."' [8] Then they went out and ran away from the tomb, trembling with amazement. They said nothing to anyone, for they were afraid.

---

[71] *The Revised English Bible*, (Oxford & Cambridge: Oxford University Press & Cambridge University Press, 1989).

THE EMPTY TOMB

Reading

The Sabbath would have ended on the Saturday evening around 6 p.m. The shops may have opened and the women could have purchased the various spices used in burial rites. Three women, probably the same three as were mentioned previously having watched Jesus die on the cross (15:40-41) go to the tomb very early on the Sunday morning to anoint the body of Jesus, and so to finish off the funeral rites that were customary for an honourable funeral and which had not been possible the day Jesus died. Obviously they have no idea or hope of what they are shortly going to encounter. They were permitted to do nothing on the Sabbath and so had to wait till it was over. On the way they began to wonder how on earth they would manage to shift the stone which blocked the entrance, but when they arrived they discovered that this very large stone had already been rolled away. We are told that the women "looked up" and saw that the stone had been rolled away. That verb has been used five times before in Mark's Gospel. Twice it refers to Jesus looking up to heaven (6:41; 7:34) and three times it has to do with "recovering sight" (8:24; 10:51-52). So, is Mark just relating a simple fact, or is there an implication about God helping the women to recover their sight, that is, their faith in Christ?[72] When the women step inside the tomb, there is a young man dressed in white. The scene might refer back to the Transfiguration (9:3) where the clothes of Jesus are transformed to be a dazzling white. Clearly this is an action of God. It is likely that Mark intends us to understand that the young man is an angel. However, it may just refer back to the mysterious young man who ran away naked in the garden of Gethsemane (14:51).

The women were utterly amazed. They experience intense emotion. Every action of God produces a reverential fear, but the young man tells the women not to be afraid, though they are not at all sure! The young man gives them some wonderful news: Jesus has been raised from the dead. The women are to go and announce this news to Peter and the other disciples and inform them that the risen Jesus is expecting them in Galilee. This had already previously been announced by Jesus in 14:28 when he predicted the triple denial of Peter. Clearly Peter and the other disciples have been completely forgiven by Jesus and he wants to gather them into a community again. It is Peter who is named individually because he played a major role in the post-resurrection appearances of Jesus detailed in the other Gospels. The flock that had been

---

[72] Nicholas King, *The Strangest Gospel: A Study of Mark*, (Stowmarket, Suffolk: Kevin Mayhew Ltd., 2006), p. 115.

dispersed will once again be gathered together and Peter will have a role of leadership in this community.

However, these women who had so bravely stood by the cross watching Jesus die are now afraid; they flee from the tomb and do not say a word. It is not clear whether Mark intends us to understand that the women were simply afraid or in complete awe at the action of God.

Biblical scholars love the next bit! From the very earliest times, people have found the ending to this announcement a bit odd. Your Bible will go on to speak of various appearances of the Risen Christ. Mary of Magdala eventually recovered and told the other disciples the news but they did not believe her at first. Hold it! Most people who know about these things say that all these appearances of the risen Jesus that we have in Mark's Gospel in our Bibles were probably not written by Mark. The scholars debate endlessly about what happened. Some say that the original ending was lost and what we have was composed to fill the obvious gap, while others say no, Mark actually intended to end at verse 8 with the women going off too afraid to say anything to anyone. The ancient tradition added what we find in our Bibles about the appearances of Jesus, and this addition has been accepted as an integral part of the Gospel, even though the final version is from more than one hand. This is not really unusual in the Bible as there are several places where we can find bits added by someone other than the original author.

The important thing is to try to understand what Mark wanted to say. Some very early writer added a bit about the appearances of Jesus so maybe the original ending just got lost. In that case we might imagine that Mark would have written something similar. However, if Mark really intended his story to end with the silence and fear of the women, what can he have meant? When he was writing, the Good News about the death and resurrection of Jesus had spread far and wide. Mark was writing for a Christian community which was suffering persecution for their faith. Perhaps he intended to show that despite our fear and reticence, the Gospel is the work of God and cannot be suppressed. However, all of this is guesswork, interesting though it might be. We do have a final part to the Gospel which has been accepted by the Church as authentic, even though it might not actually have been written by the same person who wrote the rest of the Gospel.

None of the four Gospels has attempted to describe the moment of the resurrection of Jesus. This has not stopped all sorts of people, from the earliest times, using their imagination and putting forward stories that range from the interesting to the crazy. The Gospels proclaim the reality of the resurrection but they do not describe it. There are no eyewitnesses to the resurrection, only those who bear witness to the truth that Jesus the Christ is risen from the dead. This proclamation was at the heart of the Christian message from the very beginning. Saint Paul writing to the Christians in Corinth about the year 54 A.D., before Mark's Gospel was written, said: "For I handed on to you as of first importance what I also received: that Christ died for our sins in accordance with the Scriptures; that he was buried; that he was raised on the third day in accordance with the Scriptures..." (*1 Corinthians* 15:3-4). He then goes on to list the appearances of Jesus to his followers.

In Mark's Gospel, we have the announcement of the resurrection of Jesus that comes via the mysterious young man, or perhaps angel. The empty tomb is not a proof of the resurrection but is a sign to those who accept the joyous announcement. The new community is to gather not around an empty tomb but around the person of the risen Christ. The young man/angel does not command the women to tell the other disciples to come and see the empty tomb but to go to Galilee where they will be reconstituted as a community around Jesus. Those who opposed the first Christians never seemed to deny that the tomb was empty but they gave all sorts of explanations as to why it was in fact empty.

Reflecting

Have another read of the story that we have been reflecting on in this Station.

However Mark intended to finish the Gospel, we have the joyous words of the young man dressed in white: "Do not be alarmed; you are looking for Jesus of Nazareth, who was crucified. He has been raised; he is not here. Look, there is the place they laid him." The tomb is no longer the place to find Jesus. He is risen, and through him we are offered life! In the resurrection of Jesus, the glorious state of all who remain faithful to him is anticipated.

Perhaps the fact that the women were too afraid to say anything is a reminder to Mark's own community – who seem to have been suffering great persecution – that the Good News they have must be shared despite one's fear.

The resurrection of Jesus was not the story of the resuscitation of a corpse but was about "breaking out into an entirely new form of life, into a life that is no longer subject to the law of dying and becoming, but lies beyond it – a life that opens up a new dimension of human existence".[73] The resurrection of Jesus is

---

73 Pope Benedict XVI, *Jesus of Nazareth*, op. cit., p. 244.

not an isolated event that is limited to a long time in the past but opens up a new possibility for the whole of humanity as we move into the future. We are called to a new kind of life. God's plans for us are indeed for peace and not for disaster.

Perhaps the following questions might help you to see the relevance to your own life of the scene we have been looking at where the young man or angel announces that Jesus has been raised from the dead.

1. What does the resurrection of Jesus from the dead mean to you?
2. The women wondered who would roll away the huge stone for them. What is blocking you?
3. The women were afraid to tell anyone what they had seen and heard. How do you get over your fear of living your faith in public?

Salome's account

I can remember those days very well. We were absolutely shattered. We loved him so much. He brought good news from God. Why did they kill him? We saw him die on the cross. We were determined to stay till the bitter end and so we watched where he was buried. I thank God that there was someone to give him a decent burial place. We wanted to be with him to give him some comfort in that awful place but we had to leave as the Sabbath was about to start.

We talked amongst ourselves and we decided that as soon as the Sabbath was over we would return to anoint his body with the customary oils and perfumes. After everything he had done he deserved an honourable burial and everything had to be done so quickly when he died. As soon as the market opened we bought all that was necessary and then we set out. It was only when we were nearly at the tomb that Mary remembered the huge stone that blocked the entrance. How could we shift it? Then we saw that someone had shifted it before we got there. We were very frightened and I certainly thought that someone had stolen the body of Jesus. We held on to each other as we approached the tomb, and when we entered ... when we entered we saw this man who told us something amazing. The body of Jesus had not been stolen but had been raised! We ran away! We were dumbfounded. Obviously we got over our fear but the news was so earth-shattering it took some time. Jesus is Lord! In him all people are invited to sit at the banquet in the Kingdom of God. What are you waiting for?

THE EMPTY TOMB

Responding

The resurrection of Jesus does not mean that Jesus returned to the same kind of life that we are living now. He was the same but very different. Saint Paul tried to explain to his converts in Corinth that the resurrection of Jesus meant that all of us were destined to rise again. He used the idea of a seed that is sown in the ground and then what is produced is very different:

> ^{42} So it is with the resurrection of the dead. What is sown is perishable, what is raised is imperishable.
>
> ^{43} It is sown in dishonour, it is raised in glory. It is sown in weakness, it is raised in power.
>
> ^{44} It is sown a physical body, it is raised a spiritual body.
>
> <div align="right">(<i>1 Corinthians</i> 15:42-44)</div>

We cannot grasp this with our brilliant intellects but only by faith firmly rooted in love. The resurrection of Jesus from the dead is the reason why the whole of the New Testament was written. Perhaps this Station raises all sorts of questions in your heart. Now is the time to share what is in your heart with God.

Take all the time you need.

Resting

Read again slowly the Scripture passage we have been using for this Station.

At the beginning of the Easter Vigil, the *Exultet* is sung. This is a song of rejoicing at the resurrection of Jesus from the dead, and reminds us that God had prepared for this over the whole course of the Old Testament. In this hymn, we hear:

> *This is the night when Jesus Christ broke the chains of death and rose triumphant from the grave.*
> *What good would life have been to us, had Christ not come as our Redeemer?*
> *Father, how wonderful your care for us!*
> *How boundless your merciful love!*
> *To ransom a slave you gave away your Son.*
> *O happy fault, O necessary sin of Adam, which gained for us so great a redeemer.*

The very first Christians had to struggle with why Jesus had died on the cross, and in the light of his resurrection from the dead they were able to trace God's purposes from the very beginning of the Bible in the story of the Fall when God promises a saviour (*Genesis* 3:15). They reinterpreted all the Scriptures from the standpoint of the resurrection. They saw how the psalms spoke of Christ and they understood the prophecies in the Prophet Isaiah which referred to a mysterious figure known as the Suffering Servant of the Lord (*Isaiah* 42:1-9; 49:1-6; 50:4-11; 52:13-53:12).

The New Testament is written from the standpoint of faith in Jesus as the Risen Lord. All the stories that Jesus told and all his miracles took on a new and deeper meaning. He came to bring Good News, that all of us are invited to share in God's own eternal life. Even nailing God's Son to a cross could not force God to reject humanity. Instead God responded to this rejection by offering us even more.

God has a plan of salvation for humanity to share the divine life with us. In prayer we consciously open ourselves to this new life. Gradually God enters and brings light to our dark places. At every step on the journey we have the possibility of turning away from life. Perhaps we prefer darkness to the light. However, if we decide to continue, God will lead us. In prayer we open ourselves to God's transforming action in our lives whereby our very limited human ways of loving are transformed into divine ways. Prayer has to go along with a willingness to respond to what we become aware of. We have to actively dismantle our false self, which is the work of a lifetime. Without prayer we will never have the insight to do that.

Perhaps at the end of this way of the cross, following Jesus in his Passion and death, you could spend some time quietly in God's presence. Consent to what God desires to do within you. God is offering you an invitation to the wedding feast of heaven and earth, of God and humanity. Do not miss the opportunity. God is offering you life. Take it.

What's Next?

Life triumphs over death; love triumphs over hatred. Each day we come across negative situations or negative people. In a letter St. John of the Cross wrote:

> *Where there is no love, put love and you will find love.*[74]

Try to put that into practice today.

---
[74] Letter 26, in *The Collected Works of St. John of the Cross, op. cit.*

*'Behold I make all things new' (Revelation 21:5).
Ceramic by Adam Kossowski
in the St. Joseph Chapel at Aylesford Priory.*

SELECT BIBLIOGRAPHY

Raymond E. Brown, *The Death of the Messiah – From Gethsemane to the Grave: A Commentary on the Passion Narratives of the Four Gospels,* The Anchor Bible Reference Library, 2 vols. (London: Geoffrey Chapman, 1994).

> *The* study on all aspects of the passion and death of Jesus from the historical point of view.

John R. Donoghue, S.J., & Daniel J. Harrington, S.J., *The Gospel of Mark*, Sacra Pagina Series, vol. 2, (A Michael Glazier Book published by Liturgical Press, Collegeville, Minnesota, 2002).

> This whole series is excellent and the volume on Mark's Gospel does not disappoint. It is technical but repays study.

Nicholas King, *The Old Testament – A Translation of the Septuagint*, Volume 3: The Wisdom Literature, (Stowmarket, Suffolk: Kevin Mayhew Ltd., 2008).

Nicholas King, *The New Testament – Freshly Translated with a Cutting Edge Commentary,* (Stowmarket, Suffolk: Kevin Mayhew Ltd., 2004).

> Nicholas King's translation will help the reader understand the Bible in a fresh way.

Nicholas King, *The Strangest Gospel: A Study of Mark*, (Stowmarket, Suffolk: Kevin Mayhew Ltd., 2006).

> This is a small commentary but packed with helpful indications to understand Mark's Gospel better.

Joel Marcus, *Mark 8-16: A New Translation with Introduction and Commentary*, Vol. 27A The Anchor Yale Bible, (ed.) John J. Collins, (New Haven & London: Yale University Press, 2009).

> The author published the first part of the commentary on Mark's Gospel in 1999 and the second ten years later. A great deal of scholarship has gone into this work, but a particular text can be checked without reading the whole volume.

Denis McBride, *The Gospel of Mark: A Reflective Commentary*, (Dublin: Dominican Publications, 1996).

> Excellent commentary that is what it says: reflective.

SELECT BIBLIOGRAPHY

Brendan Byrne, *A Costly Freedom: A Theological Reading of Mark's Gospel*, (Collegeville, Minnesota: Liturgical Press, 2008).

> This is the third in the theological commentaries of the Synoptic Gospels by Byrne. Anything by this Australian Jesuit is excellent and very readable.

Pheme Perkins, *The Gospel of Mark: Introduction, Commentary and Reflections in The New Interpreter's Bible*, 12 vols., (Nashville: Abingdon Press, 1995-2002), pp. 507-733.

> This is very much based on Brown's study.

Joseph Ratzinger, Pope Benedict XVI, *Jesus of Nazareth - Part Two, Holy Week: From The Entrance Into Jerusalem To The Resurrection*, (London & San Francisco: Catholic Truth Society & Ignatius Press, 2011).

> This is the second volume of the Pope's book on Jesus from a biblical perspective. He believes that the search to find the "real" Jesus cannot only be done from the point of view of history but that faith must play an important part. The Scriptures are not merely human words but are the Word of God in human words and therefore in order to understand them, they must be approached with faith.

Donald Senior, C.P., *The Passion of Jesus in the Gospel of Mark*, The Passion Series, 2, (Wilmington, Delaware: Michael Glazier Inc., 1984).

> The author has written about the Passion in all four Gospels in four separate volumes. This detailed examination of the account of the Passion is intended to lead readers to experience the power of the story.

Dennis Sweetland, *Mark: From Death to Life*, Spiritual Commentaries Series (New York: New City Press, 2000).

> This is a good commentary on Mark's Gospel that emphasises our reaction to the Word of God.

Herbert Thurston, *The Stations of the Cross: An Account of their History and Devotional Purpose*, (London: Burns & Oates, 1906).

> Interesting if you want to find out more about the early history of the Stations of the Cross.

N. T. Wright, *The Resurrection of the Son of God*, Christian Origins and the Question of God, vol. 3, (London: S.P.C.K., 2003).

> This is a monumental work that covers the story of the resurrection of Jesus in the New Testament. He sets the scene by outlining how pagan and Jewish peoples understood the afterlife and then examines the evidence in the New Testament and other works around the time. In our present work, our particular interest is in pages 616-31, where Wright deals with Mark's account of the resurrection.

Tom Wright, *Mark For Everyone*, (London: S.P.C.K., 2001).

> Same author as above. This is a much simpler book and is one of a series where Wright explains different books of the New Testament. He uses his vast knowledge of the New Testament to explain in a few words the fundamental points of Mark's Gospel. He gets the reader involved in the story by asking us to reflect on important questions as we go along.

Tom Wright, *The New Testament for Everyone*, (London: S.P.C.K., 2011).

> This is a new translation of the New Testament by a very important modern Scripture scholar who believes that each generation needs to re-translate the Bible as language evolves.

The Carmelite Family in Britain

The Carmelite Order is one of the ancient religious orders of the Roman Catholic Church. Known officially as the *Brothers of the Blessed Virgin Mary of Mount Carmel*, the Order developed from a group of hermits in thirteenth-century Israel-Palestine; priests and lay people living a contemplative life modelled on the prophet Elijah and the Virgin Mary. By the year 1214 the Carmelites had received a *Way of Life* from Saint Albert, the Latin Patriarch of Jerusalem.

Carmelites first came to Britain in 1242. The hermits became an order of mendicant friars following a General Chapter held in Aylesford, Kent, in 1247. Nuns, and lay men and women have always played a major part in the life of the Order, and have had formal participation since 1452. Over centuries of development and reform, the Carmelites have continued their distinctive mission of living 'in allegiance to Jesus Christ', by forming praying communities at the service of all God's people. The heart of the Carmelite vocation is contemplation, that is, openness to and friendship with God, pondering God's will in our lives.

Like the spirituality of all the major religious orders (Benedictines, Franciscans, Jesuits, etc.), Carmelite spirituality is a distinct preaching of the one Christian message. Carmelites blend a life of deep prayer with active service of those around them, and this apostolate takes many different forms depending on the time and the place Carmelites find themselves in.

Over the centuries 'Carmel' has produced some of the greatest Christian thinkers, mystics, and philosophers, such as Teresa of Jesus (of Avila), John of the Cross, and Thérèse of Lisieux (three Carmelite 'Doctors of the Church'). In the twentieth century, the Carmelite Family bore witness to the Gospel in the martyrdoms of Titus Brandsma, Edith Stein, and Isidore Bakanja.

England boasted the largest Carmelite Province in the Order until its suppression at the Reformation. The British Province was re-established under the patronage of Our Lady of the Assumption in the twentieth century. There are communities of friars, sisters and lay Carmelites across England, Scotland, and Wales. Similar communities exist in Ireland, and throughout the world. The international Order of Discalced (Teresian) Carmelite friars, nuns, and laity is also present in Britain and Ireland. Members of the Carmelite and Discalced Carmelite Orders work, live, and pray together to make up the wider 'Carmelite Family', which seeks the face of the Living God in parishes, retreat centres, prisons, university and hospital chaplaincies, workplaces, schools, publishing, research, justice and peace work, counselling, and through many other forms of ministry and presence.

Further sources of information on Carmelite spirituality include:

John Welch, O.Carm.
The Carmelite Way: An Ancient Path for Today's Pilgrim
(Leominster: Gracewing, 1996).

Wilfrid McGreal, O.Carm.
At the Fountain of Elijah: The Carmelite Tradition
(London: Darton, Longman and Todd, 1999).

Johan Bergström-Allen, T.O.C.
Climbing the Mountain: The Carmelite Journey
(Faversham & Rome: Saint Albert's Press & Edizioni Carmelitane, 2010).

Website of the British Province of Carmelites
www.carmelite.org

Carmel on the web

The British Province of Carmelites
www.carmelite.org

Aylesford Priory, Kent
www.thefriars.org.uk

National Shrine of Saint Jude, Faversham
www.stjudeshrine.org.uk

Corpus Christi Carmelite Sisters
www.corpuschristicarmelites.org

Discalced Carmelite Family in England, Scotland & Wales
www.carmelite.org.uk

Irish Province of Carmelites
www.carmelites.ie

Anglo-Irish Province of Discalced Carmelites
www.ocd.ie

Association of Discalced Carmelite Nuns in Great Britain
www.carmelnuns.org.uk

Carmelite Forum of Britain and Ireland
www.carmeliteforum.org

Carmelite Institute of Britain and Ireland
www.cibi.ie

International Carmelite Index
www.carmelites.info

The Carmelite General Curia
www.ocarm.org

CITOC – Carmelite Communications Office
www.carmelites.info/citoc

Carmelite N.G.O. at the United Nations
www.carmelites.info/ngo

Edizioni Carmelitane
www.carmelites.info/edizioni

Domus Carmelitana, Rome
www.domuscarmelitana.com

American Province of the Most Pure Heart of Mary
www.carmelnet.org

American Province of St. Elias
www.carmelites.com

Australian Province of Carmelites
www.carmelites.org.au

The O.Carm. – O.C.D web portal
www.ocarm-ocd.org

The Carmelite Institute of Britain & Ireland (CIBI)

offers distance-learning courses in Carmelite spirituality, history and culture.

CIBI was established in 2005 by the British Province of Carmelites, the Irish Province of Carmelites, and the Anglo-Irish Province of Discalced Carmelites.

The purpose of the Institute is to diffuse the charism, heritage and spirituality of 'Carmel' through part-time distance-learning courses in Carmelite Studies at introductory and more advanced levels.

The Institute's scholarly but accessible programmes are open to members of the Carmelite Family and anyone interested in the field of Carmelite Studies.

Through its interdisciplinary courses and activities the Institute offers an opportunity to learn about Carmelite life in its many forms, as well as a means to grow intellectually, spiritually and professionally.

CIBI's programmes – ranging from an *Adult Education Diploma* to a *Masters in Carmelite Studies* – are accredited by ecclesiastical and secular institutions of higher education, giving professional qualifications to those students who opt to submit assessments.

Thanks to the founders and sponsors of the Institute, programmes are made available to students at very reasonable rates, with a certain number of bursaries awarded to deserving individuals.

Though based in Britain and Ireland, CIBI enjoys close links with study institutes, libraries and heritage projects around the world, and welcomes student applications from any country.

For further information and a prospectus, please contact:
The Carmelite Institute of Britain & Ireland
Gort Muire Carmelite Centre, Ballinteer, Dublin 16, Ireland

☎ +353 (0)1 298 7706   Fax +353 (0)1 298 7714
E-mail: admin@cibi.ie
Website: www.cibi.ie

Other titles available ...

Also by Joseph Chalmers

A Deeper Love (London & New York: Continuum, 1999) – with Elizabeth Smith.

In Allegiance to Jesus Christ: Ten Conferences on Carmelite Life, (Rome: Edizioni Carmelitane, 1999, reprinted 2004).

Mary the Contemplative, (Rome: Edizioni Carmelitane, 2001, reprinted 2004 & 2007).

In obsequio Jesu Christi: The Letters of the Superiors General O.Carm. and O.C.D. 1992-2002, (Rome: Edizioni OCD, 2003) – with John Malley & Camilo Macisse.

The Sound of Silence, (Faversham & Rome: Saint Albert's Press & Edizioni Carmelitane, 2007).

Carmel – School of Prayer, (Rome: Edizioni Carmelitane, 2010).

Let It Be: Praying the Scriptures in company with Mary, the Mother of Jesus, (Faversham & Rome: Saint Albert's Press & Edizioni Carmelitane, 2010).

Also available in the Carmelite Bible Meditations series

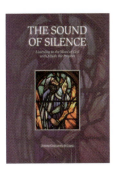

Joseph Chalmers, O.Carm.
The Sound of Silence: Listening to the Word of God with Elijah the Prophet

Joseph Chalmers, O.Carm.
Let It Be: Praying the Scriptures in company with Mary, the Mother of Jesus

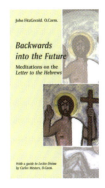

John FitzGerald, O.Carm.
Backwards into the Future: Meditations on the Letter to the Hebrews

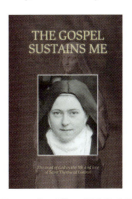

Johan Bergström-Allen, T.O.C. & Wilfrid McGreal, O.Carm. (eds.)
The Gospel Sustains Me: The Word of God in the life and love of Saint Thérèse of Lisieux

These and other titles on Carmelite spirituality and history can be ordered from:

The Friars Bookshop	Saint Albert's Press	Edizioni Carmelitane
The Friars	Book Distribution	Via Sforza Pallavicini, 10
Aylesford	Carmelite Friars	00193 Roma
Kent	P.O. Box 140	Italy
ME20 7BX	ME20 7SJ	
United Kingdom	United Kingdom	
☎ + 44 (0)1622 715770	☎ + 44 (0)1795 537038	
E-mail: bookshop@thefriars.org.uk	E-mail: saintalbertspress@carmelites.org.uk	E-mail: edizioni@ocarm.org

www.carmelite.org/sap   www.carmelites.info/edizioni

LAUS DEO SEMPER ET MARIAE